THE OUTSIDE LOOKING IN

My Life Within The Music World

Sheila DeChant

20 A-M Productions, LLC

In sweet memory of
Samuel Shep Barish
Ruth Weinstein
George Barish
Lucky, Lady, Sarah, Kasey, Kayla and Kip

INTRODUCTION

Hello to my readers.

I have always wanted to try and write a book about this unique life and journey that I have been on. I will try to remember as much as I can, so please be patient with me. Most people who follow Daryl Hall and John Oates will not remember me other than being "Mrs. Causal," married to the sax, flute, keyboard and background vocalist for over 43 years, "Mr. Casual" Charlie DeChant. I have lived and seen the life in the music world. It has not been an easy lifestyle but quite an amazing experience that has left me sometimes excited, exhausted, upset, and sometimes sad. I would call this a "musical roller coaster," which became a natural part of my life.

I hope I don't disappoint the readers about the negative side of the music industry, but just like any other business, it has its bad side and its beauty, as well. You will get a better understanding of my background and a completely different point of view of what I love the most in this world beside my husband, children and grandchildren, which is the hearts and infinite sounds of "music."

I am writing from my own personal experiences of what I have seen and done over the years. I am hoping you will like reading about the world that I was a part of, and from a different perspective. My story will hopefully leave a small mark in this world with more understanding of what it takes to be in and around the music business in hopes my daughters, grandchildren and readers will get to understand me a little better reading about what it was like from my point of view and of what I experienced.

So sit back and have a glass of wine or your favorite drink and enjoy my journey. I do feel we are all special, different and unique, yet we experience so many things that are similar. In childhood we have confusion, to having a family experiencing difficulties and how we try to overcome them. We have illnesses from a cold to certain medical traumas you can and probably will experience. We must all find a way to be happy and feel good about one's self and try to obtain self-worth as we grow. I do believe we are all connected, but we each have to find our own ways by learning and respecting the many cultures and religions that we may not necessarily agree with. But we can learn without prejudice and can respect what works for each person. Most of all, to do what you love and to be happy. Easy to say, but for some of us, paths take crazy turns some for the better and some that hit road blocks.

TIME AND CHANGES

By Sheila DeChant

I wish you love
I wish you good days
I wish you good feelings

When you've been waiting
Just for the right moment
To make the big move
That will change your life

I can recall the times
We were so unhappy
We start to blame each other
For unlucky times

But time has taught us well
Don't try so hard it will come
Just show yourself with pride
It will bring happiness inside your- self
I wish you good feelings

When you been waiting
Just for the right moment
To make that big move
That will change your life.

ACKNOWLEDGEMENTS

I would like to thank my dad, Samuel Shep Barish, for introducing me to music, even though he did not know how much music meant to me in my younger years.

To my husband, soulmate and best friend – "Mr. Casual" Charlie DeChant -- who introduced me to an exciting life filled with amazing artists and sounds of people I admired like Joni Mitchell. I have great admiration for the music of Crosby, Stills, Nash and Young, Laura Nyro, Minnie Ripperton, Steely Dan, Peter Gabrielle, Sharon Jones, David Bowie, James Taylor, Leonard Bernstein, Roger and Hammerstein, and Aaron Copeland, just to name a few that have inspired me in so many ways.

I was never "celebrity crazy" and I found during my years that some famous people had too big an ego for my taste, but from their point of view, it is hard to tell who really cares about you, the person, so I understand. But it would be great if celebrities could take into consideration that a lot of people are not like that.

I wanted to mention some well-known people who treated me with kindness and respect. The first person that jumped into my mind was Gilda Radner from Saturday Night Live. Also, John Oates and his wife Aimee; John Scapula, who played for Diana Ross; Paul Pesco, guitar player with Hall and Oates; Madonna; and many others, including Tommy Calton, great local [Orlando] guitar player who, at the time of this writing, just finished touring with Jon Anderson, and is a wonderful friend who respected my own musical abilities and encouragement; Richie Canata, who played with Billy Joel; Steve Sienkiewicz, an amazing local piano player who played on some of my songs; John Marsden, for helping to produce Charlie's CD's and helped me hear my songs I heard in my head come alive.

Charlie played with many musicians over the years that I got to know and admire. We were so blessed to have met so many great artists. I also want to mention Joe E. Ross, an actor from the TV show "Car 54 Where Are You." I remember when I was very young, he took time out to talk to a five-year-old on the phone. He was a friend of my dad's.

Much of our family getting together in 2020.

A special mention to drummer and good friend Eddie Zyne and his wife, Susan. He was a close friend and a wonderful drummer with Hall and Oates, The Monkees, Todd Rundgren, and other great bands. Sadly, Eddie passed away November 2018. He is truly missed. He told me once that the greatest moment in his life was to be able to play drums backing up an orchestra with Todd. We were all proud of him.

Of course, my love and devotion to my children, grandchildren and their spouses, Jon and Robert. A special mention and love too our extended family, Linda and Ed Mallinson, who are my son-in law's parents, and their family, like Herman and Mary, for being so nice to us and making family-time so enjoyable over the years. My sister-in-law Janine and her family. Always enjoy seeing them.

To my teacher, Mrs. Maxwell, who taught me to love reading. To my band directors William Ladue and Gus Perry, who had such patience with so many students. Norton Eisenberg, who taught me how to play clarinet and bass clarinet, and my piano teacher Jane Pyle for introducing me to the piano.

And lastly my husband, Charlie, who taught me patience, not to sweat the small stuff, and to try to do what you like.

MY FAMILY'S HISTORY

Most of the following information was obtained from a tape that I had asked my dad to make of his life. Other information was from the children of my father's sisters, brother, and my sister Loretta.

Great grandpa Borach Barish was married to Malke Rachel Rosenthal and they had four children. One of the siblings was Gershon Barish, who was born in 1870 and died in 1938. He was my grandfather. My brother George was named after him. My grandmother was Yente Fayge Rosenthal, who was born in 1874 and died in 1941.

The places where they were born were very vague. Most likely the birth country was Poland. I am still doing research to see If I can get the exact locations. The family were Orthodox Jews, so the marriage was arranged, but luckily the two of them fell in love. I hear the city of Odessa is where some of my family members were born. Others were born in Lithuania.

Yente had no education since girls were not allowed to attend school, and so they were very poor and became servants. My grandfather owned land and planted fruit trees to sell and make a living while working on his farms. He also served in the Russian military. He was able to attend school learning to read Hebrew and Yiddish but did not know English at that time. He was excellent in Math and also worked as an auctioneer.

Before he left for America, Gershon and Yente had five children who were my aunts and one uncle: Anna, Rose, Minnie, Celia and Abe. I do remember them fondly even though they passed away when I was quite young. I saw early movies of my aunts walking and strutting down the street in the Bronx, N.Y. and they were so funny to watch. I remember that my Aunt Minnie was very well endowed and always made me laugh. Aunt Lily, too. I think that is where I got my sense of humor from.

After living in a small house on East Ninth Street in New York City for quite a while, he sent for the family. There were five children and two parents living in one bedroom, a living room and a tiny kitchen, and there was one bathroom down the hall for all of them. Soon after they settled in New York, Gershon and Yente had two more children. That was my dad, Samuel Shep Barish, and my Aunt Lily.

Gershon worked very hard as an iceman and then he went into the junk business. Later, he died of Leukemia.

My grandmother had only one relative we knew about by the name of Hymie. My sister remembers him but I do not. She said he was a short, thin man and only ate chicken soup. My dad said he had an IQ of 150 and had money, but later dad found out he was making money selling worms. I do not know what Yente died of.

My Mom was born on February 15, 1917 in Philadelphia, Pennsylvania. Her father, Morris Weinstein, was from Odessa and his first wife was a doctor in Russia. They had one child together named Zuzy. Morris was Governor Lehman's bodyguard.

Morris was a Kapellmeister with the top Orchestra in the Russian Army. He came from a family of millionaires who were close with the Czar. The story goes that one night he got very drunk and yelled out, "Down with the Czar!" In order to save his life, the family had to pay 50,000 rubles to get him out of Russia which brought him to America.

In America, he met Fannie Reiss and soon they were married. He became a dress designer for the movie stars and her mother was his dressmaker. They had four children together, my mother being the youngest.

When my mom was four-years-old, her parents divorced and she ended up living in New York where her father owned a nut and fruit store. Later she was sent to live with her mother in Philadelphia so she could eventually complete her college education. Mom was only 14-years-old and only lived with her mom for one year and then went back to live with her father who, at that time, owned a candy and soda shop in the Catskill Mountains.

It was at this time that Mom saw a musician playing on stage in the Catskill Mountain Resort and she knew right then and there she was going to marry him. She was only 16 at the time. That musician was my father, Samuel Shep Barish.

MY FAMILY

My father was a physical therapist and a professional musician playing tenor saxophone, clarinet, violin and some piano. He had five sisters and one brother. His sister married Al Katz, who was also a professional musician. He and my dad had a band together called the" Al Katz Orchestra." They performed mostly in the Catskill Mountains, which is a beautiful mountainous resort two hours north of New York City. Later, after he married my mother, he moved to Outwood Kentucky near Dawson Springs where my brother was born and then to Atlanta, Georgia where my sister was born. He then became the band leader at the famous Biltmore hotel in Atlanta Georgia. He always believed you should have a backup plan in case the music bustiness didn't work out.

When we moved to Miami because of my brother's asthma, I would go with my mom to take dad to the airport where, during the fifties, you could go right up to the plane and feel the powerful engines' strong winds blowing in our faces, almost pushing us back as my dad left for New York University to become a physical therapist. After graduating, he became the head physical therapist for the Veterans Administration Hospital in Coral Gables, Florida where I was born and grew up.

He, of course, continued playing music on the weekends, mostly in Miami Beach with a very popular band director in those days. I am referring to Mal Malkin, who got my dad jobs playing with such famous artists as Frank Sinatra, Al Hirt and other celebrities that came into town. They all worked at some of the most famous hotels like the Fontainebleau and the Eden Roc. When I would drive with my dad, he liked to smoke a pipe and he would ask me to fill his pipe with this sweet smell of tobacco. I still remember the smell.

During the week my dad worked at the Veterans Hospital which today is now a famous resort, The Biltmore Hotel. The hospital had one of the largest pools in the world because it was used for the Veterans coming back from the war for rehabilitation. It also had two diving boards and while dad was working, I would swim there. My sister used to babysit in some the apartments at the top of the hospital. Once, she took me with her to babysit. I still remember clinging to the top of the hospital where you could hear the spooky wind blowing through the top part of the building. It felt haunted and it gave me the chills.

The atmosphere of the hotels that my dad played at were so colorful. Dad would sometimes take me with him to his gigs. I normally had to wait in the lobby of the hotel because I was not allowed into the nightclubs at my age around 7 or 8. I would watch the beautiful women walk by in beautiful long gowns and diamonds.

When my dad would finish playing, he would take me downstairs of the Fontainebleau to the ice cream shop for chocolate ice cream, hot fudge and whipped cream. I was in heaven. I still remember the shop and watching all the people walk by the shop.

My Mom and Dad met in my grandfather's candy soda shop in the Catskill Mountains where my mom worked. At the time, my Mom was around 16-years-old and my dad was in his mid-20's. They were married soon after they met.

My mother was very smart. She earned her degree in teaching and went to the teachers' union meetings even after she retired. She was very short at barely five-feet tall; she could barely see over the steering wheel of her car. For example, Charlie used to hold on to the door handle for dear life when my mom drove. She loved using the brakes constantly, especially when getting close to traffic lights. Stop, go, stop, go, it drove us crazy. I remember her as being very nervous and hyper so she made me feel nervous and hyper. I guess that is where I got my anxiety from. Children are very impressionable at that age and, of course, I didn't understand her behavior.

Mom told me once that she used to sing and dance in a chorus, but besides that, she never said too much about her childhood -- other than her mom married quite a few men. I never knew all the details. She left school at the end of junior high to work at a factory, and after that, she studied on her own. In Miami at the age of 40, Mom received her high school equivalency diploma and then attended and completed undergraduate work at the University of Miami. She graduated in three years with only one point under Cum Laude [which is high honors] and then went on to receive her master's degree in education.

My father, Samuel Shep Barish.

After 30 years of marriage to my dad, she wanted a divorce. It was very hard on all of us, but after my sister and brother left, I was confused and didn't know what was happening. We ended up moving a few times, so it was a rough time for all of us as a family.

When my mom was in her 80's, tragedy struck our family. She decided to buy a car and then tried to park it in a garage above her apartment and couldn't do it. Thankfully, it was time for her to stop driving. She took the car back to the dealership and started taking the bus to the teachers' union meeting even after she retired.

I was home in Orlando when I got the news. My sister called me and said that mom was standing at a bus stop in downtown Miami across from her teachers' meeting. We are not sure of the exact details, but it was a 85 -year old woman with an elderly gentleman seated next to her. Either they didn't see my mom standing there, or my mom was off the curb. Either way, the woman hit her with their car and ran her over.

My sister called to say that Mom was at the trauma unit and had an accident and that she did not make it.

You can imagine how shocked I was. A few days later, I went down to Miami and went with my sister to the police station to get some of the things she was wearing at the time of the deadly accident.

My brother, George Barish, was 11 years older than me and four years older than my sister. He was a workers' compensation lawyer who also did very well when he invested in a small strip mall and then sold it. George was married before to Edie Garfinkle. They had two children: Robert Barish, who owns two stores and has a stepson Jake; and his daughter Marilyn Audet, who works in billing and has two sons – David, who we call DJ, who is studying auditory disabilities in Seattle and Portland Oregon, and Seth, who is currently working at a bank. The marriage to Edie did not last, but years later, I introduced him to my vocal teacher, Sheila Marchant. More about them later.

Me with my brother, sister and mother.

Sad times for George and our family began in the early 90s when he visited my brother-in-law, an optometrist, for an eye exam. There, a shadow – that turned out to be cancer – appeared in one eye. It had progressed to the point that surgery was immediately needed to remove the eye; an artificial eye was inserted. He had a wonderful sense of humor about his fake eye. He said, "wouldn't this freak people out if I went down a water slide into the pool and my eye popped out?" I could just imagine seeing an eye floating in the water with a grin on his face. I am glad that didn't happen but I did snicker at the thought. A few years went by and sadly the cancer had spread to his liver. George was taken to Dana Farber Cancer Institute in Boston where he almost died when his white blood cell was at critical levels. He amazingly got through this event and was able to come back to Miami. A few years went by and sadly the cancer had spread to his liver.

During this time is when Hurricane Andrew slammed into the middle of South Miami in 1992 with wind speeds of up 175mph [category 5]. In Wikipedia they described Hurricane Andrew as a small Cyclone and being the costliest disaster at that time in the state's history and the United States. My brother's house had a lot of damage. I heard at one point they had to brace their legs against the front door as the wind power almost pushed the door into the house. I remember coming down a few days later with water seeing a giant tree pulled out by its roots, and an apartment complex nearby with the whole front of the building torn off, and you could see each apartment.

My brother, who was an attorney, then built a small strip mall which was sold. Years later, he helped to produce my sisters-in-law's record. He stayed at my sister's house while Sheila, my sister-in-law, dealt with repairing the house.

I came down to see my brother from Orlando after starting a new job at Disney World. He was laying in my sister's back bedroom where he was on morphine and sometimes would come out into the living room. I had to leave that day in 1993 because of my new job at Disney World and he asked when his son, Robert, would come. I told him that he was flying in on Friday and he looked at me in a daze and said softly, "that's too late." I didn't know what to say. I drove home which took me about four hours and when I got inside my house there was a phone message from my sister to tell me that my brother passed away right after I left. I felt terrible that I left. It was a hard time for the family, especially when we were still dealing with the affects of Hurricane Andrew which devastated the whole area.

My sister, Loretta Francis Barish Morris, is seven years older than I am, and was closer to my brother, who was four years older than her. She was a teacher and after her marriage she became an optician. She is married to Dr. Stephen Morris, who she met in summer camp during the high school years.

Dr. Morris is now a well-known optometrist winning quite a few honors in Miami, and was also the Florida Optometric Association president for many years. He was the eye doctor helping the Miami Hurricanes, and he and my sister do some annual work for the Hite Foundation for the blind. They have three children:

Debbie Brockway, who is an elementary teacher. She is married to Chad, who used to work in management for Don Shula's Restaurant but now works for Orkin Pest Control so he could have weekends home with their son, Cooper. Cooper was at Parkland High school in Parkland, Florida when the mass shooting took place on Valentine's Day, 2018. Chad also has a daughter, Haley.

David Morris, who is a doctor with a business degree and has three daughter's, Berkley, Blake and Brennan.

My sister's third child is Darlene, who is a real estate agent and married to Jose. She has a stepson, Andreas.

GROWING UP IN CORAL GABLES, FLORIDA

My name is Sheila Diane Barish DeChant. I was born on May 27, 1949 at Jackson Memorial Hospital in Miami, Florida. I was told by my mom that my heart was out of place and I had a heart murmur. However, it did not seem to affect me as I grew up. I did have some asthma, for which I was given Ventolin to keep it under control. I also developed Spondylolisthesis which is a spine disorder in which a vertebra slips forward at a certain degree onto the bone below the low spine.

In my childhood, I developed grade three slippage but as an adult my spine had fused -- so now, I have grade two, which is a good thing.

I sometimes seem to have a strange gait when walking, but no one said anything except my dad, who kept on telling me to stand up straight – which, you would think that as a physical therapist, he would have noticed that something was wrong, which in later years, he finally realized.

I loved the city of Coral Gables where I grew up in the 50s. I lived there until I married in the mid-70s. Coral Gables is located on the west by Red Road and north of Sunset Drive, West 49th Avenue and Old Cutler Road and south of Sunset Drive, which is bordered by Douglas Road and 26th street and also my street, Palermo Avenue and La Jeune Road.

Coral Gables was founded in the 1920s by a developer, George Merrick, who had envisioned a beautiful community near the sea but, unfortunately, he passed away before his dreams became a reality.

The project was taken over in the 1950s when Colonel Robert Montgomery and his wife, Nell, lived in the neighboring area call Coconut Grove [which is where I met my husband]. He added many palm trees but he ran out of room and ended up buying the south part of Coconut Grove known today as Coral Gables. He is famous for such landmarks as the beautiful Fairchild Tropical

Gardens [which is used as a research and teaching center]. Thousands of visitors come to see the amazing Florida treasure and landmark even today. The large grand entrances into Coral Gables were built mainly of stone, including the street markers around the 1940s. One of the main landmarks is the Biltmore Hotel [which I will write about a little later] including the Venetian Pool and Miracle Mile.

One of my favorite childhood places was the Venetian Pool, where I spent a lot of my time as a child swimming with friends and family. Venetian Pool is an historic public swimming pool which was completed in 1924. It was originally known as the "Venetian Casino" that was built out of coral rocks on four acres of land. The pool was also made by George Merrick, adding to the idea of a Mediterranean style throughout Coral Gables theme. It was designed by artist Denman Fink, replicating the feel of Venice, Italy with a Venetian bridge and mooring posts. The Venetian was visited by many celebrities in the 1940s and 1950s, including Johnny Weissmuller, who was the first Tarzan, and Esther Williams, a competitive swimmer-turned-actress. An island was created representing the docks in Venice and a high diving board was constructed on top of a beautiful waterfall. The diving board was eventually taken down because of safety concerns. An interesting piece of history was that the pool would occasionally be drained so the Miami Symphony could perform in the pool. You could then hear the natural acoustic sounds that surrounded the pool. Restoration of the pool took place over the years as needed and in 1981 the Venetian Pool was added to the National Registry of Historic Places.

When my family moved to Coral Gables, my father had a house built ranch style in a middle-class suburban neighborhood for about $55,000. In 2020, I found out it was sold for almost $1 million. The house was white with dark shutter and three giant mango

The Venetian Pool.

trees in the back yard. The trees sizes were large, medium and small. Of course, when I was little, I named them Dad, Mom and Baby trees. I loved to climb the trees and sit up in the branches looking at the sky. I loved being up there. Years later, my father decided to tear down the trees and put in a pool.

I sure did miss the trees. I was sad when they were cut down, but I did enjoy the pool.

The house had three bedrooms up two step, all on the same side of the house overlooking the pool and earlier before the trees were cut down. My parents were down the hall with their own bathroom. My brother's room was in the middle, and my sister and I shared a room toward the back of the house. We all shared the same bathroom that was in the middle of the bedrooms. We had a small living room but mostly we gathered one step down to the family room. Toward the front of the house was the kitchen with a door leading to the garage. The front of the house had a long narrow patio with bushes lined up across the patio and one step down to the walkway.

I am sure my sister was not too happy when she got older that she was sharing the room and bed with me. I did have a playful spirit, and I remember that I played a little kid joke on her. We were in the bed sleeping and one night. I slowly moved my hand on my sister's back and I yelled "roach!!" and oh, what a sight it was too see her jump and run out the door. I am sure she was quite mad and I did not know why I did it, but I do like to make life there fun and those were happy times for the family.

I had an imaginary friend who you might remember from the early Disney shows -- "Zorro," who was a Spanish fictional character created in 1919. He was a masked bandit who fought for the poor but had a dual personality as a snobby rich man who kept his "Zorro" identity a secret. One day I marked a "Z" on the side of my bedroom end table. My Mom was really mad when she saw the mark, but I kept telling her that Zorro did it. She, of course, did not believe me but I did. Yes, I really dreamed he was there. I also loved the character from the show "Swamp Fox" starring Leslie Nielson who played an American Revolutionary War hero, Francis Marion. I am so glad he went on to do some great funny movies like, "Airplane," and "The Naked Gun."

I loved to go to my neighbor's house down the block and they had these small sour orange trees called Calamondin fruit that I loved to eat. The fruit made your mouth pucker every time you would eat one because they were so sweet and sour at the same time.

I also loved to get coconuts from the palm trees growing around our neighborhood. In time I got quite good at opening them up with a screw driver and peeling away at the hard-outer part and then breaking the shell and drinking the sweet coconut water and eating the coconut meat inside. Sadly, years later, Miami had some kind of infestation that destroyed most of the Coconut Palm trees, but today, thankfully, they are growing back. Unfortunately, there are not as many as they were in the past.

Since my dad was a physical therapist, he sometimes brought home an electric wheel chair and I loved to ride it and go up and down the street. I always tried to find different things to keep me interested and I guess this was one of them.

Another childhood place I would visit a lot was a 630-acre Park called Matheson Hammock. It included a large man-made pool that was surrounded by a beach and the Miami intercoastal where we could see fish and hermit crabs, a park, marina and a undercover restaurant surrounded by boats on the other side docked at a near-by pier.

Here I am at three-years-old.

My friends would go to the end of the block in an empty wooded lot where there was a mystery tree house built in the middle of the lot and there were hundreds of butterflies that we would catch. We never knew who built that house but it was so much fun to play in there and imagine that we were stalked by pirates or running away from the bad guys.

What was so beautiful were the many big orchid trees growing all around our block with bright and colorful purple and white flowers. I wonder if they still exist?

My childhood friends were Sandy, Carolyn, Lenore, Valerie and Mary. To this day I don't know where anyone is except Sandy. She and I have been friends for over 60 years, but she lives in Boca Raton now. We would get together and play all kinds of imaginary games from riding on pretend horses to building boxes into ranches for our toy horses we bought.

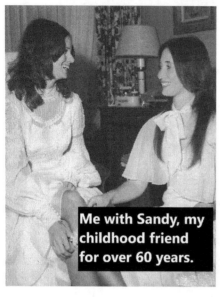

Me with Sandy, my childhood friend for over 60 years.

Carolyn lived a couple of blocks from me in a beautiful white two-story house and down the street from Sandy. We all thought her house was haunted and we were sure we saw things moving at the front window of her house. We definitely had a wild imagination and we swore we saw Carolyn's white lady statue move.

Carolyn's dad had something to do with race horses at Hialeah race track and once in a while her dad would take all of us very early in the morning to the race track so we can be with the these amazing, racing thoroughbreds. I remember the wonderful smell and playing in the big pile of hay.

We would walk into the stable and you see these majestic beasts and how graceful they were on and off the track. We would go eat breakfast around sunrise and then we would hang out some more at the stables pretending each of us would own part of a horse, and, of course, guess what part I got? Later we would play in the hay and rolled around awhile. I really liked it there and wanted a horse of my own so bad.

One of my best memories is when my parents would take the family to the beach. I would watch my brother and sister horsing around with each other and run around in circles around me. I tried to participate but I couldn't keep up. And since I was much younger, I gave up and started watching them have fun. But I felt left out. Just watching was a big word for me because I could not participate in a lot of family activities due to the age difference. That is one of the reason's I titled my book, "The Outside Looking In."

One time down the block of my neighborhood, I had a problem with these boys who lived a few doors down from my friend, Lenore, who I often went to visit. Anyway, as I was walking to her house, one of the boys threw a rock and hit me in the back of the head. Crying, I ran home and my mom was in her room typing. I told her what happened while she was working and not looking up at me. At first she said to stay away from those boys, and the next thing I knew I was feeling something wet going down my back. My Mom finally turned around and saw my whole back covered with blood coming from my head. Instead of stopping the bleeding, she grabbed me and pulled me down the block to the boy's house, yelling at the parents. Lenore's Mom came out and got me since she was a nurse and stopped the bleeding. I always wondered why my mom didn't take care of my injury first.

My first experience with death was of my dog, Lucky. I loved her so much. She was a big comfort to me, and was my best friend. She was a mixed gold and white collie, and we had her for seven years. I remember we were outside when a bunch of dogs were in my neighborhood and one of them bit me on the cheek. I think Lucky almost got into a fight with the dog that bit me, but I don't remember. The whole family loved her, and she was my constant companion as my sister and brother got older and into high school. I was pretty much by myself then, except for when I was with Lucky.

Lucky, at age seven, started getting sick and she eventually stopped walking. My dad kept her in the garage while she laid on a blanket, so I stayed with her almost all the time, staring at her and hoping she would walk again. Lucky had liver cancer. My dad would take her to the vet quite frequently and then bring her home. One day, he came back without her. As you can imagine, I was so heartbroken. To this day, I still remember Lucky with great love and fondness.

I was also close to my family's maid, Emma. I didn't really think of her as a maid and I really cared about her and she really liked me. She became my comfort while everyone in the family was busy with their lives at school and work.

Sometimes I would play tricks on her like I did my sister but she never got mad. I was always happy to see her, but when she left after my parents' divorce, it left me even lonelier and sad. I didn't understand why she had to leave. I was never told she was leaving. She was great comfort and the color of her skin never made any difference to me.

I still don't understand to this day the horrible judgement people make because of skin color. I found that quite stupid.

I am sure people are not bad because of the color of their skin. Years later, I think back and realize that no one in my schools had dark skin. Being preju-

My brother, George, with my mother.

dice was there, I guess, but well-hidden from kids. Later I found out that Emma became a teacher. My Mom told me, but I never saw her again and I missed her a lot.

My neighborhood felt safe and we pretty much knew all of our neighbors except one that lived next to the house across the street from us. I would look outside my bedroom window and I would see this huge overweight man in his boxer shorts watering his lawn and dancing. His name was Mr. Sullivan. It was a funny sight, and he looked very strange to me. Then one day I saw him outside and a police car drove by. He got in and I didn't see him again for a long time.

The house Mr. Sullivan owned was eventually purchased by a nice Lady and her children. One day I saw them running across the street to our house. She said," there's a man in our living room, he just walked right into our house, said hello and sat on the couch!" We found out it was none other than Mr. Sullivan who was drunk and thought he still lived there. The police were called and he was taken away. We never saw him again after that.

My father had a red and white boat. One of the happier times is when the family went out to the intercostal waters of Key Biscayne surrounding downtown Miami. We would go all the way to the side of Biscayne Park where a man would be near the docks in the back of the park selling hot roasted peanuts. We got close to the dock so that dad could get us a bag and while we traveled down the waterway, we enjoyed the taste of the warm peanuts. It made the boating experience enjoyable.

I do remember my father coming home one day from a boat trip. He said he had caught a large fish and told us that he and my brother had caught a shark that they pulled into the boat and had to hit with a hammer before it could bite either of them. I was sure glad that I was not on the boat when that happened.

I started school at Temple Judea, which was a few blocks away from my house where Mom would drop me off every day in our station wagon. Since I was only five-years-old, I don't recall it that well, but I remember liking it there. I do remember my mom taking me one day and accidentally leaving the passenger door slightly open. Back then, kids those days could sit in the front. She started driving to the school and the door flew open and I fell out. I don't think I was hurt, but it is funny how you remember little parts of your life in bits and pieces.

I started at Coral Gables Elementary, where I was taught by one of my favorite teachers, Mrs. Maxwell. She taught me how to love reading. I did so well that I was always asked to read to other classes. I really enjoyed that.

Every morning, the students would walk across the elementary school to the candy store. Sometimes, parent would give us money to get what we wanted. My favorite was the sweet red waxed lips you could put over your mouth and later eat it. "Yum!" I thought. Other treats were Sugar Daddy's [which was a hard-Carmel lollipop], Lik-A-Maid [which look like different color small crumbles candies], Peanut Butter logs, small waxed bottles fill with syrup, Cream soda, root beer, candy gum cigars, Milk Duds, Sugar Babies, etch. I wonder if any of you remember those. We loved that store. I was so skinny then that my mother didn't care what I ate as long as I was gaining weight.

My other famous places were Royal Castle Hamburgers, which is similar to White Castle but so much better, followed by Root Beer. To this day we still go to Miami and eat at Shorty's Barbecue for their smokey ribs, corn soaked in butter and their famous cole slaw. For special occasions we used to drive to Miami Beach to the Embers Restaurant.

I have to mention Wolfies on 23rd Street off of Collins Avenue in Miami Beach. It was a landmark until 2002. The restaurant was open 24 hours a day and was famous for overstuffed sandwiches like pastrami, matza ball soup, stuffed cabbage, borscht, cheesecake and other Jewish traditional foods. Such famous entertainers would eat there like Milton Berle, Henny Youngman and even some mobsters.

PLEASANT DREAMS

By Sheila Dechant

Gracious me, what did I dream?
I finally found the end of the rainbow
It ends in a wishing well
Snow White, Cinderella and Bambi all together
I woke up smiling and remembering

My dreams full of wonderful delusions
Hours I spent with my own illusions
Pleasant Dreams to all
Breathe good air for a change
Wonderful memories
Remember your fall, winter, or spring?

I was sitting alone watching the stars.
When Peter Pan came to my side
He took my hand and we flew away.
I woke up smiling
It made my day

There were times that I would walk a few blocks down across the street from my nursery school. There was a Russian ballet school there and I used to watch the dancers all the time. I loved the way they moved. It seemed like they were walking on clouds. I wanted to be a dancer, but I guess because of my spine I was not encouraged to try ballet or jazz.

At home, when no one was around, I would play around with my dad's piano and dance through the house and listen to music. I did not let the spine issue stop me from trying to dance. The music surrounded me like someone was hugging me, and it felt like I was floating. Unfortunately, I did not know I had a spine problem then. No one was ever sure if my spine disorder came from the old days when they use to pull babies out with forceps when they were born, or if it started when I was older. I was riding a horse and I was near a fence and some trees that hung over the fence. I stopped near the fence and trees for a minute, and suddenly one of the trees cracked apart and my horse bolted. I heard a small crack sound in my back when that happened. I remember the feeling when it happened but I don't remember it hurting.

The first five or six years of my childhood were happy times, I thought, except for the rigid punishments if I did something wrong. At that age, like most children, we have innocent minds and trusted family completely. But, in those days, you did not have the right to question your parents. You did as you are told, or there were severe consequences. I always would ask my father "why" and he did not like that. My father's punishments could be quite severe. I could not understand why I could not say what I felt or believed. The more I questioned, the harder the punishment -- and he would not stop until I cried. Remember in those days, children were seen and not heard. I did not understand this.

As time went on, I started becoming more withdrawn and more shy. Since I was the youngest, the family kept most things going on within the family a secret from me. We are of the Jewish faith and my parents only spoke Yiddish when they did not want me to know things. Later, I sensed that problems were occurring between my parents. I really did not understand what was going on. I am sure they thought it was the best for me to not know, but the atmosphere was so uncomfortable around them and I knew something was not right. I think that is when I started having stomach issues, which did turn out to be from both nerves and gastro reflux [which was medically diagnosed years later when I was an adult]. Children can sense things and I felt something was terribly wrong.Since I had to go to bed way before my sister or brother had to, I still would watch through my bedroom window what my sister and brother were doing without them knowing. Just remember the age difference kept me apart from the sibling activities. It left me lonely a lot of times. I saw my sister being picked up by her boyfriend [who is now her husband, Steve] or just hanging by the pool at night.

I wanted to say that I was not very good at changes, and stability was so important to me, but that all fell apart when my parents divorced. I became very scared and confused.

Me with my
father in 1955

As a child, I was not allowed to say what I felt, and if I did, I was punished and felt anger all the time, mostly toward my father. I was never allowed to make choices on anything that was relevant to me at the time.I had ideas and thoughts, but because of my young age, it didn't matter. Maybe it was because of how far apart I was to my sister and brother. I always wondered if I was an accident,t but my sister said no. How would she know, I thought? If I wasn't a surprise, the neglect and impatience that was happening towards me was very much felt. My shyness took over, but I was still very stubborn.

I do know that I will always struggle with this insecurity that was instilled in me at an early age, but I am still trying to really believe in myself. I am not a quitter. So today, I would say I battled the evil and won ... but it sure did take a long time to get to this point in my life.

It was a few years later after I was born that my parents started having emotional issues. They did not have a lot of patience with me. They had two older children, and then had to start all over again with a baby. Today, I can see why they were like that, and maybe you, the reader, can, too. The routine of a happy home-life was no more for them.

As for me, I felt scared and alone.

This next poem I wrote because of the inner secrets going on within my family.

WHISPERS

By Sheila Dechant

Close your eyes and listen closely
Of people who travel in shadows
Using others to bring out their sorrows
By the way they whisper
By the way they whisper

As the years drift slowly by
You find yourself dreaming
Of what you should have done
But you feel people's whispers
That left you walking alone
In the sand, in the sand

As you stare into the water
You go back to your lover of the past
Seeking the answers
You find your faults in those whispers
That left you staring in their eyes
Whispers can destroy us
If we let people control our lives
Don't listen to the whispers

I had a cousin, Alice Gottlieb, who was about my age. She would come over to swim or I would go to her house. This was when the Beatles first began playing. She really liked them, but I wasn't crazy about them for a long time till I got older. I did like the Rolling Stones. She and I would sit out on the swing set at her house and listen to all kinds of music. Years later, Alice moved to the Boca Raton area and then moved somewhere in California, so I never heard from her again.

Our family took a car trip to the Bronx, New York to see my aunts and my Uncle Abe. It was an apartment close to the Bronx Zoo on Union Port Road and I remember climbing stairs to a quaint apartment, where I was given a room to myself in the back.

I do remember coming down to the front of the apartment and seeing my three aunts walking up the walkway and dancing like in a chorus line to the apartment. They were so much fun to watch. The only person in the family that was close to my age was Peter Blankfield. I thought to myself that it was great to finally have someone I could relate to. Before I went to bed one night, he came in and gave me some paper to draw on and said good night to me. I was laying in the bed and hearing the strange sounds you don't hear in Miami. I'm talking about the subway trains loudly passing by every so often. I still remember about the sound which made me feel a little scared for some reason, but I fell asleep.

The next day we went to an amusement park with Peter and the family and we had a lot of fun. My cousin, later in life, became the lead singer and composer with the J. Geils Band, and he changed his name to Peter Wolf. He recorded hits like "Centerfold" and "Freeze Frame." Many years later, I was watching my husband record at Criteria Recording studio in Miami and, as I was sitting on some big boxes, I looked down and one of them said "recordings by Peter Wolf." It turned out to be quite a coincidence. Quite a while after that, we were eating at a Hall and Oates dinner with a large group of people and I found out Peter was there, too, but I did not see him.

When I was living in Orlando. I found out that Peter was playing with his band at an outdoor concert about 30 minutes from my house, so I went to see him. Just as I was walking to the side of the entrance to the concert, Peter was in a car with some other musicians. I yelled to him and told him who I was. He said, "Oh, Yeah, you're George's sister, I will leave you some tickets for the show," and he drove off. I was left standing in the middle of the parking lot, feeling hurt that he left like that. I just wanted to talk to him, to see how he was doing and catch up with family. I ended up not staying for the show, as I was feeling sad and confused at his reaction, so I drove home. I did talk to some people who were part of the Hall and Oates road crew and some musicians who worked with Peter, but I no longer wanted to contact him. It seems we were around some of the same people, but it didn't matter.

Also, around that time, we got to see the 1964 World's Fair in Flushing Meadows, New York. This was an amazing event, looking at what the future would look like, such as cars, appliances, etc. I still have some clippings of the fair.

We also went to see my mom's brother, Uncle Irving, who was very wealthy, and I was told he was one of the innovators of the Astro Turf. We went to this highrise in New York City and sat on pillows in this big apartment overlooking the city and we ate Japanese food. It was the highlight of my trip. He was also a funny man like my aunts and I liked him a lot. We also went to a famous Italian restaurant, "Mama Leones," which was the best Italian food I ever ate.

Years later, when I moved to New York and was pregnant with my daughter, Jennifer, I did get to eat there one more time, but, sadly, the restaurant closed after that.

This was also the first time I got to see Broadway shows like, "Unsinkable Molly Brown," with Debbie Reynolds and Robert Preston, who also starred on Broadway and in the movie version of "The Music Man." Later in years, I also saw Carol Channing in, "Hello Dolly," "Cats," "Chicago," with the great dancer Anne Reinking, David Bowie in, "The Elephant Man," Frank Langella in "Dracula," and Yul Brynner in his last performance of, "The King and I." Broadway was so exciting with the bright lights and colorful stage productions in those days.

OUCH!!!

When I was around seven or eight, I though I was invincible and that I could do anything. I would not let my spine be an issue and keep me from being active. I started by climbing up our big mango trees then jumping over the bushes in front of my house, and ended up breaking my collar bone.

Me at nine-years-old.

I remember pulling my mother's typewriter, which was on a rolling table, down the steps to the family room. I pulled it with the table behind me and it ran into the back of my heel. Blood was pouring out of my heel. I ended up at Children's Hospital emergency room because I hit an artery. The doctor put some numbing medication into my heel to stop the pain but I guess it didn't absorb enough and I ended up screaming. I am sure everyone in the hospital must have heard me. Anyways, they eventually stopped the bleeding and repaired the artery.

SCHOOL DAYS AND ACCIDENT-PRONE

After Coral Gables Elementary, I went to Ponce De Leon Junior High, which was close to the University of Miami. My favorite subjects were science, social studies and physical education, but I was struggling in math. Surprisingly, I did well in algebra. I remember where this teacher in social studies would come to each of our desks, and every time he would bend down to look at my work, these flakes would come down onto my paper. I later realized it was dandruff. Talk about disgusting.

The saddest part of junior high was sitting in class and hearing the announcement that President John F. Kennedy had been assassinated on November 22, 1963. The teacher made the announcement so we watched the news that afternoon.

In junior high was one of the biggest events in my life [at that young age]. The Physical Fitness program at Ponce De Leon Jr. High had a lot of sport events, so I tried out for different running and jumping events. One event was the 600-yard dash. My mind was made up that I was going to win one event, and I knew the dash had to be it for me. Most of the girls were in eighth or ninth grade so I entered against some great runners, but I was so full of energy and excitement that it didn't matter.

The whistle blew and my feet moved before I could even think. You could hear everyone running beside me, but I kept my eyes straight ahead and felt myself reaching as hard as I could toward the finish line. My breathing became louder and I quickly glanced over and saw Diane Taggert getting ahead of me. I felt this sudden urge to push as hard as I could as the finish line was closing in.

The announcement came five minutes later that Diane and I had tied for first place. I felt so proud of my accomplishment, even though the odds were physically against me. Diane and I received an award and our names were published in the school newspaper. Go, Sheila!

Would you believe the very next day I tried the trampolet, which is a small round springboard and you can run, jump up and bound off of it and even do somersaults in the air and backward flips? I really liked doing it until one last try, I landed on my arm and my arm went limp. I ended up with a fracture. I remember standing in the hall as a safety patrol for the school and my arm was strapped to my chest for support. It is a good thing I didn't try it before the 600 yard dash.

At first, my father did not believe I broke my arm again, and kept me in bed for two days with my arm laying on a pillow. Finally, he took me for an x-ray and, sure enough, my arm was broken. I never lied to my dad, but he just had a hard time believing me.

To end this chapter on a good note [no pun intended], my dad took me with him on a road trip to the west coast, including the Grand Canyon, Las Vegas and Los Angeles to see Beverly Hills and Disneyland. I really enjoyed the trip and my favorite place of all of them was the Grand Canyon.

Dad booked a mule trip down to the bottom of the canyon. It was pretty scary going around all the mountainous downward paths and being on the edge of the cliffs as the mules slowly moved like it was just another day at the Canyon. I must admit that it was a wonderful trip.

THE TEENAGE YEARS

It was not talked about, but I know when I was around 15 that something was still wrong with my parents and I guess that was when their problems started escalating. By this time, my sister Loretta and my brother George were married and out of the house.

In 1965, I started at Coral Gables High School and began taking lessons in clarinet and bass clarinet. I did like the band, and I had a really good friend, George Grummet, who played trumpet. We used to talk almost every day in the music locker room before the band started. He was such a good friend to me with a great sense of humor. I finally found a friend, and we talked a lot -- but nothing romantic happened. It wasn't that kind of relationship.

One day I found out that something happened to George. I was told that he was on the football field and fell to the ground. Later, I found out he had a heart attack at his young age and passed away. I was devastated. I had never known anyone who had died before, with the exception of my dog, Lucky. I never talked to anyone about George's death because I did not have too many friends who knew George. I still, to this day, remember him fondly.

Like I said, I only had a few friends in band, but my parents wanted me to join a Jewish group. However, I did not feel comfortable with any of the girls. They were very cliquish and I thought, quite truthfully, that they were snobs. I had made friends with the head baton twirler, Darlene Lunquist. She was quite beautiful with blonde hair and a really nice person, but she was a few years older than me. We did a lot of shows since the school was a very prestige school, yet it was a public school. We marched a number of times at the Orange Bowl and did concerts and some parades. The one thing I hated was marching with the bass clarinet, it really hurt my neck a lot.

This was the time when my hormones were kicking in. The interest in boys started. I had two crushes: Arnold, who was then a senior drum major while I was a freshman. A drum major is the head of the marching band directing with a long baton while marching in front of the band. He looked so great and I guess he was my first crush. Another band member I really liked was Clayton, and he played trumpet. We became friends after George passed away.

It seems I got along better with boys then I did with girls for some reason. I thought they were less emotional and more confident, or so I thought.

Marching and concert band was my whole life at the that time. I learned a lot of music from Broadway show tunes to the classics like Aaron Copeland and Igor Stravinsky. This was a great time too study the different composers, and some of the melodies were so beautiful. I remember hating the low bass notes I had to play at that time. I wanted to be playing clarinet more, or even learn flute.

Around the end of my second year of high school when I was finally getting comfortable, things at home went from bad to worse. My dad moved out of the house that I loved, and it was put on the market. I was pretty much alone now that my sister and brother started their lives. I felt isolation and such unhappiness. It was bad timing for me as I was just starting the teenage phase.

The next thing I knew and without my knowledge or warning, Mom and I moved out to a high-rise on Brickell Avenue called "The Brickell Town House". This was close to downtown Miami and the entrance to Crandon Park and Coconut Grove. It was also near the famous Vizcaya Museum and Gardens, where years later, Daryl and John played at a private function that was mentioned in John Oates' book, "Change of Seasons."

Brickell Town House was a tall modern building in those days -- over 26 stories high overlooking the intercostal waterway. We moved to the 26th floor. The apartment was nice but felt so strange after living in a house.

The building had a pool, off the water where I would swim and sit watching the bridges and buildings of downtown Miami. I would even see dolphins swimming by. It was a beautiful place, but to me it just wasn't home. I remember getting mail for a Keith Barish, who I did not know but had our same last name, and found out later he was a famous director. I would bring his mail down to the front desk quite a few times. After settling in, I was finally told where my dad was, but it really didn't cross my mind to ask.

Since I did not live in Coral Gables any more, I had to leave my Coral Gables High School and transfer to its rival, Miami Senior High School, where I also started in the band. I liked the band members who were very nice to me. The best thing about it was that I did not have to march with the bass clarinet anymore. The band director, Gus Perry, let me march with the clarinet and

Me with my sister, brother, and favorite dog, Lucky.

just use the bass clarinet for concerts. Hooray for that. We also had a band club that I was allowed to join which was fun and the best way to meet new classmates.

I don't remember the education I got at the school. It was so vague to me, but I do remember our first band trip by train to Washington D.C. to perform for the yearly Cherry Blossom festival. It was a great time, especially being away from the drama at home. I got to be with a boy I had a crush on, Al Torrente, who played trumpet and later became a popular trumpet player in the area. I liked him a lot, but nothing romantic happened.

Living at Brickell Town House, I would have to catch a bus to downtown Miami and make the transfer to another bus to Miami High. The bus would cross the downtown bridge, but on one of the days, for some reason, the bus would drop us off a little farther down the street. I remember someone in front of me had tripped as he stepped off the bus onto the sidewalk. I was right behind the person and I stepped right into a hole on the sidewalk. I badly twisted my ankle and tore ligaments which ended up being a fracture. "Here I go again!"

My mother was getting so tired of me always hurting myself, I guess she thought I was doing it for attention. Geez!

My mom was not very happy, and her anger was getting worse and her temper was really out of control sometimes. There was one situation when, while I was watching TV, she got mad at me because it was too loud for her and she wanted me to turn it down. Well, I got mad at her yelling and I wouldn't do it. She took the back of the handle of a hair brush and started hitting me with it. I couldn't understand why she was so angry, but I must admit that I had a stubborn streak as a teenager and, of course, she was going through a hard time. I was in the middle of a marital storm and it took a toll on me emotionally.

While I was living at Brickell Town Hours, I met a friend in the building, Karen Korey. She was a little strange, but very nice. She had brown hair and was short like me. I found her interesting, so we became friends. She introduced me to this guy in the elevator that she knew, Robbie Cosby. I did not know how important he would become in my life.

Robbie was tall, thin, really sweet and handsome with dark blonde hair. It was the first time of feeling attraction toward anyone since high school and I guess he was feeling the same

My 1967 Miami Senior High School class photo

way about me, because we started a conversation that left me pleasantly surprised – which became the start of a loving relationship. We always hung out together, mostly by the pool or at his mom's house. He had a Harley Davidson motorcycle and we took rides around Miami or up to Fort Lauderdale. The wind, a kind soul behind the wheel, and a Harley. I couldn't ask for anything more at that time.

One day though, I had gotten off the bike and the side of my leg hit the burning hot engine and it was pain I never felt before. Later on, it left a scar. Robbie will always have a special place in my heart because he really helped me through the hard times when my parents divorced. He became my only support during that time, since my sister and brother were busy with their lives and, of course, my parents were too involved with the emotional turmoil of separating for good. Being a teenager, trying to find myself, eventually moving in with my dad, and then back with my mom was not fun. With Robbie with me, I thought I handled it pretty well, considering the confusion for me.

The relationship with Robbie was growing strong. He really cared about what I was going through since his mom was also divorced, so he understood. We got close to consummating the relationship. However, he wanted to wait until he could take care of me. He decided to go into the Army to build a career so that we could get together, but it was also the start of the Vietnam War.

Robbie had a hard time during basic training and he tried to get discharged because he did not believe in the war. He called me and said he tried to fake a suicide attempt by putting his hand in a light socket, but they would not discharge him. Next thing I knew, He went AWOL, and was coming to get me to go with him to Canada. I wanted to go so bad but I just couldn't do it. I knew I was just too young and that I had never been far from my family before. Robbie left, I knew I had hurt him badly, and that was the last time I ever saw Robbie again. I cried and cried, and then time went on until I ran into his sister and she said he did go to Canada, but she did not know where he was living. I always wondered what my life would have been like if I had gone too Canada with him. In the end it was the right choice, but I still think of him fondly.

There was a club I used to hang out at called "The World," where I met a boy name Jack. There were a lot of famous bands that went there, like "Iron Butterfly," and one of my favorite groups, "Spirit." I guess I was lost, searching for attention and affection or something, but I did not know what. With turmoil at home, Jack was the answer for me at that time.

Jack had dark hair almost black, slender body and deep dark eyes that seem to look right through you, and the relationship started with trips to his house in North Miami, going to the clubs or hanging out in North Miami Beach. Three years later, Jack became physically abusive to me. My dad gave me this old white car, which I think was a Chevrolet. One day, I was late driving to Jack's house and I was on I-95 in Miami. The expressway is one of the busiest highways in Miami.

As I was driving toward his house on the left side of the expressway, I see on the right side of my car that another car was drifting into my lane and I was waiting for a crash too happen. I jerked the wheel to get out of the way and I lost control of the car. The car started sliding. I hit the brakes. I just remembered riding a horse and if the animal gets out of control, you pull hard on the reigns to extreme left or right and the horse would stop. I did exactly that. I took the steering wheel and kept turning it and the car was heading toward the guard rail and I was so lucky I was not near any cars, and the car stopped inches before crashing into the rail. I was shaken but thankfully unhurt. It turned out that the axel of the car had busted and that is why I lost control.

I don't remember how I got to Jack's house, but not only did he get mad that

I was late; he slapped me for being late. This was the beginning of the end for us.

My dad did not like Jack, so my father forced me to go with him to Europe. I don't want to sound spoiled but, in my eyes, I had to leave Jack and that made me very unhappy and, at that age, the heart wants what the heart needs. I was miserable without Jack. I realized it was not love, but dependency.

I must admit, it was nice to see Barcelona and Madrid, Spain and London, where I got this beautiful emerald dark satin blouse. We traveled to Amsterdam, Germany, and Paris, where we climbed the Eiffel Tower all the way too the top. We later took a night boat on the Seine which traveled around the Eiffel Tower while we were being served Lobster. We visited other places like Rome, where we visited the art museums to see such wonders as the Mona Lisa and even The Trevi Fountain. It was not that I didn't appreciate Dad's effort to take me on this trip, but we didn't have much of a relationship. He always talked as if I was five-years-old and could never see that I was growing up, which was sad in a way. I can see now that he had older children and with the age difference it must have been hard for him to connect to me.

My favorite place we visited was Switzerland. The mountains were massive and the snow so beautiful. We took the train around Switzerland, which turned out to be the highlight of my trip.

When I got home, at first Jack was happy to see me, but the relationship got worse. We would usually hang out at a video arcade place in North Miami Beach. We were standing outside and Jack did not want me to go into the arcade with him and told me to wait while he went inside. I waited for quite a while and, finally, decided to look through the window of the arcade to see if I could find him. There, he was holding a girl's hand. I dropped him at his house, not saying a word. I was hurting at his betrayal and I never saw him again until a few years later. I decided I was going to concentrate on my music and stay away from guys.

JACK

By Sheila DeChant
He was the boy, who walked right in
And took away my heart
His name was Jack
I didn't know where he came from
He sat across the bar
Not touching his drink
He stared in my direction
He walked across the floor
Didn't ask me anything
Just took my hand
Looking at my eyes
I didn't think twice
He was the man who
Walked right out of my life
Ending up with my best friend
Now his wife
To this day I see his eyes with that gaze
In my direction
His child in his arms
The hurt in my soul
A bad dream that will slowly fade away.
I knew a man
Who walked into my life
His name was Jack
He looked in the wrong direction
He lost me forever.

LIFE AFTER HIGH SCHOOL

After I graduated from Miami High in 1967, l continued my education and went to Miami Dade South campus and studied education and music. I was in the Miami Dade chorus and studied voice and piano. I also got into ballet, jazz, tap and did some local shows as part of a dance group. I did not let my spine control my life, even though there were times could not do double turns because of balancing issues -- but I really loved to dance.

My voice teacher was Sheila Marchant, who had a beautiful voice with blonde, striking features with blue eyes and taught a lot of students how to sing. Some of the students became quite famous and were my classmates, like Desmond Child, who later wrote for bands like "Kiss" and "Ricky Martin."

She also taught a girl singing group known as the "Rouge sisters," who later backed up Gilda Radner on Broadway and who I met years later. Sheila, herself, was offered to be an understudy for the Broadway singer Shirley Jones, but they wanted her to travel on the road, and so she declined. Sheila was my vocal teach and student, friend and later, my sister-in-law. At that time, she was not married.

My brother was single again, going through the hippie stage and getting into pot. His ex-wife, Edie, was gone and took Robert and Marilyn, my niece and nephew, back to Massachusetts where she had family there. It was a heart-wrenching time for me when they left. Edie was always good to me. It was sad for me knowing I was going through my parents getting a divorce and also knowing that Marilyn and Robert were gone. It left me lonely and lost.

I introduced my brother to Sheila and he fell head-over-heels in love with her. I really did not see what she saw in him, but she felt the same way, and a few years later they were married. Now here is a strange side-note. Sheila Marchant became Sheila Barish, my maiden name -- and then when I got married, I was no longer Sheila Barish but became Sheila DeChant. Talk about irony with me and my new sister-in-law. I really liked Sheila and was so glad it was working for them. George was finally happy again until my brother passed away.

I am back-tracking in my story, but after I graduated Miami Dade with an associates of arts degree, my father really wanted me away from Jack, so I went to Florida Atlantic University in Boca Raton and lived in the dorms. I was missing Jack a lot, but I did well in some classes and joined a fraternity. I was not happy there and a little over a year later I stopped going to the school -- that is when my dad ended up taking me to Europe, whether I wanted to go or not.

Soon after coming back from Europe is when I caught Jack cheating on me. I remembered singing in my head, "Hit the Road Jack," and added "Jack got the sack."

In the summer, I went to the University of Miami Summer Band Camp and really loved playing in the concert band. When I was on campus, I mostly enjoyed going to the Music Library. The atmosphere of music all around you was wonderful. There was a part of the library where they had thousands of written compositions and records from famous composers from all over the world. The library had booths where you could go in and listen to the music or you could sit at a table with head phones with written compositions in front of you. I was able to follow the notations as the record was playing. I loved every minute, watching each measure come together and fit perfectly. It was a great learning experience for me. I got to experience such great composers, including of my favorites, Aaron Copland and Leonard Bernstein. Seeing and hearing how the music moved note-by-note was something you can't explain until you do it. It was a magical time that I truly miss.

THE MUSIC WORLD

I started going to some clubs like World and The Place, as I wrote before. That is where I also met a keyboard player, Jennifer Keyes, who was playing for a band called Fantasy. They were quite popular in the area and recorded a few albums. We became good friends and, eventually, I moved from my mom's house and moved in with Jennifer. I would go with her to shows, and that is when the world of music entered my life again. I really started thinking about singing at that time, but I did not know how to go about it and was extremely shy with no self-confidence at all. I started watching a band called, "The Bird-watchers," and I had a little crush on the bass player, Jerry. He always told me not to get involved with musicians. I was "too nice a girl to get involved."

I would watch Jennifer play a lot, and mostly watched many bands and their singers, always wishing I could do the same thing, Eventually, Jennifer moved out of the apartment and I was left alone and I started to have panic attacks and was sick to my stomach. My father came and got me. He ended up taking me to the hospital. They gave me Valium, which didn't work, and the panic got worse -- and then I couldn't breathe. I realized later that I was having an asthma attack, but was treated for anxiety, instead.

After the hospital, I moved in with my dad for a while. I felt alone, confused and depressed. I did some elementary school substitute teaching and also worked for a temporary agency called Kelly Girls. I took one job with them in the downtown area for a doctor, Sherif Shafey (sp), and I was told he was a relative to the famous actor, Omar Sharif, who played the lead in the movie, "Dr.Zhivago," "Lawrence of Arabia," and "Funny Girl." When I went into the office, one of the employers warned me that the doctor was not very nice. The employer was right. He was rude, demanding and mean, so I walked out very discouraged. I was sorry he was like that since I liked what Omar had accomplished.

I started hanging out with my friend, Karen, who at that time was dating and living in an apartment in South Miami with Frank Trabinello, who turned out to be a bass player with a famous local Miami band called "Sun Country." Frank was famous for a billboard that had his picture that said, "Get a Hair Cut." I tried to find the billboard but never could. The lead singers were Steve and Lee Tiger, who were Miccosukee Indian brothers who had different bands over the years. Their dad was a very famous man by the name of William Buffalo Tiger, who represented the Miccosukee tribe and lived in the Everglades in a tribal community until he passed away at age 94.

Karen and Frank got married but, unfortunately, the marriage did not last.

The apartment was full of talented, creative musicians, singers, and writers. Of course, some were into pot, but I am sure there were some drugs used, too. I never seemed to be interested in getting into drugs because I was mostly concentrating on singing, and I did not like taking anything that made you feel out of control. When I came to visit Karen and Frank, they introduced me to a guy named Jim. We became friends and he was into recording, so since I had been writing some songs, Jim started recording me on an eight-track machine. He really liked to record, but he also had a crush on me. However, I did not feel the same way about him. We remained friends until I met Charlie.

One of the many people that came to the apartment was a girl named Kitty. We hit if off right away. She had a beautiful voice, and still does. I really admired her singing and confidence, which I did not have. She was one of the singers in a band called Christian Gandhi Syndrome. Kitty, in later years, married George Terry, who is an American Blues rock and roll guitarist playing with such greats as the Bee Gees, Diana Ross, Stephen Stills, and many others. You can check out Kitty and George on YouTube.

These were great times for me. I was surrounded with such wonderful and talented people. I knew there was something inside me, but I never knew how to move forward to create. It was hard for me. I did not comprehend what was holding me back. I sometimes think, and I am not making excuses, that, while growing up, I was never given any kind of positive encouragement from my family on anything that interested me-- like dancing, singing, or any ideas I had. In fact, I was punished for expressing myself at a young age. I had lost something I could never get back, but it didn't stop me from trying.

If you knew me today, you would not believe how shy and intimidated I was back then. Remember, they were my teenage years, and this whole generation was lost in some ways, especially with the Vietnam War and the mandatory draft going on.

After a while, I got a job with Screen Gem Music Publishing Company. I had an interesting job where I would sit on a stool and to the right of me was a drawer filled with individual musical notes. I would follow sheet music and place the notes on the giant music boards, and then take these boards and bring them to a large photo picture room where each of these boards were photographed into sheet music -- which eventually were turned into music books.

The end of the 60s was such an exciting time for the baby boomers and such diverse music coming from every direction. I am hoping one day that this will happen again, but most likely it sadly won't. More about business than music, it seems to me.

While I was working at Screen Gem, I was sitting next to a girl named Shelly. We became friends and it turned out she was dating a famous musician, Dr. John, for a while.

We went to a club together and a group called Iron Butterfly was playing at the club, "The Place," and Shelly met the lead singer, Mike Pinera. He asked her to come to his house and, since she was nervous, she asked me to come with her. I remember sitting in his kitchen while Shelly went somewhere with Mike. I was quite naïve of where they went. Finally, she came back and seemed fine. We left, but she did not tell me what happened.

I remember my friend, Jim, took me to the University of Miami when they had bands come in to perform and one of the groups was a band called, "Bethlehem Asylum." I was not crazy about them or the music and I thought they were kind of stuck up. It turned out that one of the band members would become my husband.

"Bethlehem Asylum" musicians were made up of Buddy Helm on drums [he used to play with Tim Buckley and Frank Zappa], Danny Finley on guitar [who played with Kinky Friedman], Christian Ghandi [who wrote some of the original songs] and Jim Neiman on drums. They were signed under Ampex label and had a jazz-rock sound. The band had a great local fan base. Unfortunately, Christian disappeared years later and no one had ever heard from him again, and Jim Neiman is now deceased. The band had financial issue and eventually broke up.

During the summer of 1970, a group of us drove to the Atlanta Pop Festival where we mainly stayed in the giant parking lot with thousands of other people. We could not get close to the stage, but we still could hear the different bands playing, like The Allman Brothers, Chamber Brothers, Grand Funk Railroad, Richie Havens [who Charlie played with years later and I had met), Jimi Hendrix, B.B. King, Rare Earth, Spirit, John Sebastian [who I met years later], Johnny Winter and many more. It was an amazing festival and it was the first time I drank beer. I do not like liquor, but I was so thirsty, I drank the beer. It was cold and I thought to myself that it wasn't too bad, but I would have preferred a coke. Years later, I found out that Charlie was also at the festival, but we still hadn't met yet.

At this time of my life, I dated a few guys but ever since my break-up with Jack, I would not get close to any one for a long time. It was a bad ending and I was not looking to get involved.

I didn't mention any connection with my family at this time of my life because I never had any kind of good relationship with my siblings or my parents. I don't think you can blame me with the chaos I went through with them. I kept most things to myself. While I was living with my dad, he got me a job working for him at a private nursing home called, "Green Briar." After my father left the VA hospital, he decided the nursing home was a better place for him at the time as the head of its physical therapy department. I would help patients move their arms and legs, and help them walk and then take them to their rooms. I hated the medicine smell in the rooms, but some of the patients were very sweet and wanted to take me home.

My father noticed I had these red welts on my arm and he thought I was taking drugs and made me get a drug test. It was just allergies, but by this time, my father did not trust me at all and I gave up trying to prove myself. A lot of anger and hurt ensued. This relationship was broken like the marriage to my mom. He only saw me as his little girl that disappointed him. I had a mind of my own. With him, things had to be his way, and I couldn't accept that.

The following lyrics is about a mother and child who lived around drugs and guns like it was a normal way of life. This was showing how children saw things as they grew up in a violent environment, especially in the inner cities. This was a song that never got recorded but here are the words.

MARY AND THE CHILDREN

By Sheila Dechant
Walking down Darlington Square
Mary came to the school over there
Watching the children playing but scared
Seems like the violence has struck here
To Mary and the Children

They hear the anger from the streets
She turned around and saw their fate
What will come of them as they see?
Their parents selling drugs so they can eat
But look out for
Mary and the Children

Mary looked through the child's eyes
Saw one girl staring past
AS the gunshot flew by fast
And struck Mary's Dad

Watching the people walk away
Like this was just another day
The children went back to playing scared
Mary went home to bury Dad
It looks bad for Mary and the Children

It there's a story needing told
To keep the young ones from the old
To see the cycle, start again

Just like Mary and Her Dad
There is hope for Mary and the Children

This next lyric is remembering why I like writing words and how it feels.

My Songs

By Sheila DeChant

Finding new ways to end my day
Striving for good thing to come
Catching melodies soothing sounds
Out of nowhere
Here come my songs
I must try to know words that make you feel

Must be inside you
Right or wrong
This is the only way
To show love on my own
By playing my songs
Sensations in my mind
It's just so hard to say
What you're feeling inside
Remember your first roller coaster ride?

Music surrounds me wherever I go
Hear my fantasies, feel my soul
This is the only way, just writing my songs

My family, right before I met Charlie

HERE COMES CHARLIE

After Jack, I was not interested in getting into a relationship, so I decided to become a nun. Just kidding! I decided to concentrate more on composing and lyrics. I started writing back in 1971 and continued throughout the years, but never did anything with them for a long time. I just didn't have the confidence to find someone since I didn't think anyone would be interested.

My friend, Jim, asked me to come with him to this club so he could record this band called Christian Ghandi Syndrome at a club called The Last Word. Today, this club is an empty building along 67th Avenue and Coral Way close to Coconut Grove and just a few blocks from where my niece, Darlene, and her family live now.

I was sitting with a group of people at a table near the stage while Jim was recording the band. As I was watching the band, I was listening to the music while they were playing Elton John's "Take Me to the Pilot," a song I had never before heard but really liked. I was enjoying the band and their unique sound. After they were taking a break, the drummer, Buddy Help, came over to me and started talking. He seemed very nice, but a little flirtatious, so I was feeling uncomfortable. My bad break-up with Jack kept me from wanting to start any kind of relationship. I said to myself, "music, Sheila, just the music."

The band continued playing some really great songs, and even my friend, Kitty, was singing with them -- and she sounded great. I envied her. Then I looked up again and I saw this sax player with long blonde hair, tall and skinny, with round rimmed glasses.

His name was Charlie DeChant.

He had this sound coming out of the horn that was smooth like ice and had emotion I never heard before. I looked up at him and, when he finished playing, he looked right at me. This felt like he was looking right through me. He kept staring at me and I, without thinking, started staring back and -- Wham! Something happened. His stare from the stage across the room was startling me and I was no longer thinking. I remember saying to myself, "uh, oh... no way. I am not getting involved, too painful."

After the band took another break, Charlie came over to me and said, "are you with these people?" and I sarcastically said, "no, I am not," thinking that was a stupid question. He sat with me and we barely said anything until he asked me to go out and have hot chocolate with him. I thought about it and decided to go. Curiosity got the best of me.

Charlie did not have a car so I ended up driving him to a small place for hot chocolate. For Miami, it was pretty cold outside. It's funny, but I don't remember the conversation at all, but afterwards I drove him to a house in Coconut Grove where he was staying with the drummer, Buddy, and his live-in girlfriend that everyone called Barbara Banana.

Charlie (second from left) with the Christian Ghandi Syndrome Band

We were sitting in the car and Charlie leaned over to kiss me. I looked and him and said, "I just met you." Charlie looked at me and said, "okay, goodbye," and proceeded on getting out of the car and went up to the house. I was thinking, "well, that is that." I realized that I was attracted to him, but luckily keeping my emotions in check after a broken heart was a good thing. I was still living at my dad's house in South Miami. By now, my dad and I did not have too much to say to each other and that was fine with me.

A few weeks later, Jim asked me if I wouldn't mind going with him to record the band again at a private, elite and expensive school in Coconut Grove, Ransom High School. It was in a beautiful area of the Grove with lots of fruit, bamboo and cypress trees. I almost stayed at home, but Jim talked me into going, and I knew that Charlie was going to be there.

So here I am again, watching the band and listening to the music with my friend, Kitty, singing. I remember thinking how wonderful she was and how much I loved the sound of her voice, and the band sounded great. They were playing in the school's large gym, where people were dancing. I was standing near Jim, and there it started again. I saw Charlie, and he saw me, from the stage ... and the staring at each other happened again. I knew something was going on, but I did not try to pursue this since I did not want to be upset again.

Once the show was over, I was pacing the gym waiting for Jim to pack up the recording equipment. I was getting bored, but was peering at Charlie packing up his horn. Then, as I was turning to leave, Charlie walked right up to me and said, "do you want to go out with me, or not?" I replied, "Well, I don't know, I guess so." I was very hesitant, but curiosity got the best of me again.

He had soulful blue eyes and he loved the same thing I did, the music. I did not realize -- nor thought -- that he played the same instrument as my dad did. It was an unconscious feeling that I was not aware of at the time.

Afterwards, we ended up at a party at this big one-story house on the water in the Grove. Charlie and I sat on the deck off the glistening water. I remember that he kissed me softly. Yes, I am a sucker for romance, but I was not thinking about what was happening, and neither was he.

After a few days, Charlie called and asked me to come to a friend's place to eat, so I picked him up and we went to this girl's apartment, and she made spaghetti and meatballs. Later, Charlie told me that he had slept with her and asked if I had known that. All my dreaded feelings and emotions of "oh, no, here it goes again" started coming over me. I would have never gone there. Charlie acted like it was not a big deal. He didn't realize that it was a big deal to me.

The next lyric is after I had been with Charlie over 21 years. I hope you remember the moment you fell in love. What a rush!

TEARS OF JOY

By Sheila Dechant

When your world feels like you're falling in a dream
And the time goes so sweetly
When you feel Tears of Joy

You did not know when the moment came
We lay together whispering
And the tears came into my eyes
Knowing my life has changed

Scared that it wasn't real
Scared that you don't feel the same
You stare and just knew

You asked me if I fell in love
I said yes with tears in my eyes.
Love came in a wave so strong.
It brought me Tears of Joy

I stared in you eyes to hear some words
And you said so meekly
I feel a pull so strong
He touched my tears
Scared that it wasn't real
Scare that you don't feel the same
You stare and just knew
When your world seems like you're falling in a dream
The time goes sweetly by
When you fall in love
And you feel The Tears of Joy.

So, this is the Romance?

About a month later, I had gotten really sick with bronchitis and no voice. The beginning of a relationship was not a great time to be sick. I received a call from Charlie and he said, "hey, you got me sick." I felt like he blamed me for getting him sick on purpose and I didn't even know I was sick until a few days later. We both ended up coughing, and each had stuffy noses, which sounded funny when we were on the phone both blowing our noses and losing our voices. What a pair we were.

This was about the time when I started being with Charlie more and more and not going to the apartment as much. I really liked it there. I recall being in Karen's apartment and she had pot in her freezer and she had a Monopoly game on the table. I took a few hits and before I knew it, the game became so much fun and we were laughing and at some point, we didn't care who had what property so we were trading deeds and money, no matter who had what property. I guess you had to be there, but it turned out to be a moment that I will remember every time I play the game.

It was also the end of my friendship with Jim. He wanted more from me romantically but I didn't feel the same way. He looked so sad and I felt for him, remembering Jack's behavior toward me at the end. I just wish I could have made him feel better, but there was nothing more I could say to him except I was sorry.

I started going with Charlie to some of his shows, which I enjoyed. At this point, I was following my heart. One time I went with Charlie to a club called The Possum in Coconut Grove, and it was upstairs in a large bar and club with a large crowd. The band started to play and I was so into the music. The musicians, including Charlie, started ad-libbing these different sounds of jazz rhythms with the melody coming in and out of these off-the-wall movements, and then Charlie started playing these licks. He got so emotional playing his horn, like he was going crazy, and I started getting emotional and was worried that he was freaking out. I ran out of the club pretty upset, not knowing why or what he was doing. I didn't understand. Later, he went looking for me and found me standing outside of the club. I did not tell him how upset I was.

Our relationship grew, and Charlie moved out of Buddy's house into a one room place connected to a large beautiful house, still in the Grove. We often hung out in his room while he played his guitar. The view was really pretty outside his door, with lots of hanging tree and a fountain surrounding the yard. We were laying together and I remember the time I started crying. Charlie asked me if I was in love with him. I started crying harder and nodded. I really was fighting this feeling, especially when I had experienced my own loss, and my parent's divorce. We held each other, saying nothing, and so our journey truly began.

If you remember reading about my parents not getting along, divorce was eminent. I was not happy staying at either of their houses. I did not belong anywhere and, truthfully, at that time Charlie had moved again to a house in the Grove with his two friends, Randy and Cathy, who were really good singers and song writers. They had two bedrooms and a dog. This was when Charlie and I decided to move in together. The house was small,l but we all learned to live together for a while.

Charlie did a lot of different shows and I let my music take a back seat because of the relationship we were building. Yet I still had a desire to sing and compose and was hoping maybe Charlie and I would do something together in the future. We did try once, which ended in a fiasco for me.

Charlie was playing in a club and the band was playing, and I got up to sing "Proud Mary." The band never asked me for the key I wanted to sing in, so the whole song fell apart and I got off the stage and left upset and crying. Charlie would not talk about it.

At this stage of my life, I was in love and not thinking of anything else. It took work to stay together. I hoped that, maybe in the future, I would be able to sing and compose again.

Charlie was so involved with me and his music. It was confusing at times for both of us, but the attraction we had for one another was really strong. Like any true relationship you remember having, I would call it the lust stage – and it really was.

I went with Charlie to Key West. At that time, the Key West airport had a club and Christian Ghandi Syndrome were offered a chance to play there. It turned out to be a very strange night for me.

I was sitting at a table in the club when this girl, who was with her parents, sat down with me at the same table. It turned out she was Charlie's ex-girlfriend. So here I was, with Charlie playing on stage and his ex-girlfriend watching him play. I really got very uncomfortable and confused, so I walked outside not knowing what I should do. I got into our van that was parked in front of the club. I had very mixed feelings from anger to hurt at this encounter and kept staring at the front door of the club.

Charlie and I have some really good friends who played guitar, including Kip and his brother, Jonathan. They had long, messy red hair and beards, but what nice guys they were to me. Well, Kip had come out of the club a little while after me because he saw what was going on and the situation I was in. Being the great guy he was, Kip did this funny and wonderful thing that I was not expecting. He stooped down next to the car so I wouldn't see him, and the next thing I knew, I saw bubbles floating across the windshield… lots of them. At first, I thought I was seeing things, and I laughed so hard. He made me feel better. He was so sweet. I never forgot his kindness.

Charlie did not seem that concerned about this ex-girlfriend showing up at the club as we drove back home, and he acted like nothing had happened. He did that a lot when he didn't want to talk about things. I felt confused about the situation and tried to forget about it, too.

Sadly, year later, Charlie and I found out that Kip was in the Bahamas at some person's house, and we guess there were drugs involved, and Kip got shot and was killed. We were so sorry to hear about that. I think his brother, Jonathan also passed away a few years later of an illness, but I am not sure how he died.

There were times that I didn't go with Charlie for a few days. Mostly because I needed my space and to work on myself a little, but then again, I got both of us kicked out of Randy and Cathy's house.

There was this guy who walked around the Coconut Grove area, staring inside people's houses, and he was known as "The Creeper." I was alone, except for Randy and Cathy's dog that was roaming the house. My sister lived about 20 minutes from the Grove, and she had a Great Dane puppy named, Duchess. I asked her if Duchess could stay with me while Charlie was gone because I was afraid of "The Creeper," who could one night be looking into my window. Duchess would stay with me in the bedroom, but Randy and Cathy's dog kept

Me & Charlie, some time in the mid-70s.

coming into my room, which almost resulted in a dog fight. Cathy gave me an ultimatum to either remove Duchess or we had to go.

I had to break the news to Charlie when he came back from Key West and we ended up moving out of the house, which was a good thing for us. It was time we found our own place.

We found a temporary place, still in Coconut Grove, with a drummer who was renting a house. His nickname was "Mouse." But don't ask me why, except he had this thick, afro hairstyle and played drums really loud -- but he was very nice. He gave us a room, but this was not really a room, it was more like a long narrow closet with a bed. I remember him practicing his drums from the other side of the wall.

After a few months, we got a small one-bedroom apartment attached to a house, still in Coconut Grove on Shipping Avenue. You walked into a tiny living room and to the right was a really small, narrow kitchen. You reached a small bedroom from the living room, or you could walk around the corner back to the kitchen from the bed. It was our first place to ourselves. There was a ladder that you can climb up to the roof, with lots of tress surrounding it, where Charlie would play the guitar and we would look at the stars. It was nice up there. Reminds of when I used to climb up my mango trees at home.

We could walk a few blocks to the water and sit down by the cement wall surrounding the inlet while Charlie played and we talked. The view, I must say, was very romantic.

Coconut Grove, at that time, was so filled with energy, music and artists. The park near the water with anchored big boats and sail boats, and a lot of performers would show their many talents right at the park surrounded by the inlet.

The 60s and the 70s were a great time to be in the Grove. There were some famous musicians and singers that came here and played in a wonderful club called The Flick. This is also the place Robbie used to take me to, and was ten minutes from where we lived near the University of Miami.

The Flick Coffee house in Coral Gables opened in 1963, but closed down 10 years later. Names like Joni Mitchell, John Sebastian [who I had the pleasure to meet years later], Jimmy Buffet, Crosby, Stills, Nash and Young, Tim Buckley, John Denver, Gamble Rogers, Vince Martin, Terri DeSario [who sang with KC and the Sunshine Band], and a favorite local musician, Bob Ingram. It was not a big place, but the atmosphere and music were electric. Gabe Kaplan from the hit show, "Welcome Back Kotter," hosted a three-day event for its 50 birthday at the Flick. It was a special place for all of us.

The co-star of "Welcome Back Kotter" was Marcia Strassman, who later dated Daryl Hall. She was very nice to me, but we did not hang out since she lived in another state.

Another special place was the Vizcaya Museum and Gardens, also in the Grove. This beautiful estate was owned by businessman, James Deering of the Deering-McCormick international Harvester fortune, which opened in 1916 with an area of over 130 acres. The architecture was a combination of Baroque architecture, Renaissance and Mediterranean style. In 1935, a major hurricane hit Miami and caused major damage to the estate. The estate is also a museum where events are held including concerts, weddings and tours of the museum.

In John Oates' book, "Change of Seasons," he writes about the Hall and Oates show he did at Vizcaya, where I also attended. While growing up, Vizcaya was also an intricate part of my life.

Another of my favorite places I would go to since I was three-years-old was Shorty's Barbecue, which opened in 1951 starting as a barbecue stand then a restaurant. Shorty's original owner was Edward Louis Allen, who died at age 104. The restaurant burned down in 1972 but was rebuilt in the same place on South Dixie Highway. It is still here to this day, and every chance we get, we head right for Shorty's.

Charlie also was playing at the local clubs. One time, he had a gig at the club, The Place. They had pinball machines, and competitions for highest score, of which I won a lot. This was where Jack and I had met.

Charlie was playing one night, and I really liked to dance there. One night, I saw Jack there, and he saw me. He came up and just started holding my hand like nothing happened. Well, I put a stop to that and pulled my hand away and told him that I was with someone now, and I walked away. The song, "Hit the Road, Jack" was playing in my head as though it was written for me.

By this time, I wanted a dog. Charlie and I went to the Humane Society and got a puppy named Jazz, but sadly the puppy ran away and we never found her. Then we went back to the Humane Society and this guy was dropping off this black and white puppy, which was a Border Collie. We saw her, and the guy gave the puppy to us. We named her Lady. With Charlie coming and going, it was nice to have Lady with me.

We enjoyed our little one-bedroom apartment, but one night we were sleeping and, for some reason, I woke up. At the end of our bed, against the wall where our TV was, a giant water rat was literally on the wall. He was scary and climbing the wall. I jumped and pushed Charlie off the bed and just pointed. I won't tell you what expression Charlie had, but you can guess. He went after the rat, not knowing what to do, but then the rat just ran around the room into our kitchen. It must have run up the pipe underneath the kitchen sink and disappeared. We never saw him again, but the next few nights I was very nervous.

The second incident was when we came into the apartment to our bedroom. As I was sitting on the bed, for some reason, I looked up and was staring at the sky through the roof right above me. There was a big hole in the ceiling, with plaster on our bed! We called the manager and found out what happened. The owner had a worker on the roof and, as he was walking, the part of the roof above our bed caved in. Can you imagine if we were sleeping in the bed when that happened? I was so glad we were not in the bed at the same time.

My dad really liked Charlie, and of course they had a lot in common, but he didn't like us living together so he never came to visit us. However, my brother, after his divorce, would sometimes come over. He was living the single life. He was trying to find himself, so I hope we helped him a little, especially when I introduced him to my voice teacher and it turned out to be a great match.

LEAVING THE GROVE

After four years of living in our small but comfortable apartment, we moved out of the Grove. We went 15 minutes away to South Miami and rented a large house, but did not live there very long. The house was nice and had a piano in the living room, but then we were offered a mobile trailer home in Homestead, but did not want to live so far away from the Grove.

We finally found an apartment in the Kendall area called the Sunset Apartments, near my sister's house, where we finally settled and started meeting other people who were not part of the music business. The apartment building had about 100 units, and we chose a two-bedroom which was nice. It overlooked the pool that was in the center of the complex and off the streets of Kendall Drive.

Our first friends were Bruce and Peggy, who lived a few doors down from us. Peggy was a bubbly blonde, almost six-feet tall, and Bruce was much taller at around six-foot-three. We hung out a lot and she had quite a personality, which made being with her a lot of fun.

Charlie and I had been together for four years and I was getting frustrated that he never proposed to me. I finally brought it up, but he ignored me. Well, one day we were going to one of his shows in Key West and, as we were in the car at a strip mall across from our apartment, I had enough and needed an answer.

I was scared but I decided either Charlie wanted to commit, or I was leaving him. His way of ignoring issues did not work this time and I stated that either we get engaged now or I was going to leave him.

I started getting out of the car. He looked at me and said, "well, I am scared." It was funny that he should say the same thing that I was feeling. I told him that I was, too. But what's the point of staying together if all you're going to do is trudge along? Charlie agreed.

I guess he did not want to lose me, and we loved each other. I knew in my heart that I would have left for good, even though it would have been really hard for me, and thinking ahead on where I was going to live.

It was pretty confusing, that conversation we had. It was not the most romantic way to decide to marry but at least he agreed. We were both worried about the future, especially since the music world is always financially very risky. There was no bending of the knee to propose or an engagement ring. No! I can't make excuses for him or my low self-esteem issues, and maybe I should have walked away, but one thing was for sure -- the love was there for us both, even if he didn't admit it.

We got married on April 4, 1976 on my sister's birthday, even if we originally wanted to get married on April Fool's Day -- but the date wasn't on a weekend. So we picked April 4th and chose to be married at my sister's house, since it had a huge back yard and porch and, of course, it saved us money.

Loretta's house was a one-level Florida-style home with a large family room with glass doors that went out to the back yard. Our wedding day was exciting for both of us. I decided on a light cream-colored wedding gown that I had rented, and Charlie matched with a cream colored tuxedo that he also rented. We figured that we would only wear them for one day. He looked awesome. I had my childhood friend, Sandy, and some other good friends [who were mostly musicians] and their wives at the wedding. It was also a rare moment when my father and mother were together for the wedding.

April 4, 1976

We couldn't afford a professional photographer, so our wedding pictures were not the best, but at least I still have some.

As I got ready in my sister's huge bedroom, I drank wine. I usually didn't drink, but as we say, "it's a special occasion." I could hear Charlie out in the living room playing his Sax, and my dad joining him on his clarinet.

My siblings all won scholarships in music to the University of Miami band, including my brother-in-law. In those days you could study other areas and still get a scholarship through the band.

Meanwhile, I would listen to my dad and Charlie play until it was time for me to go.

When I got outside to walk down the aisle, the beautiful flowers on either side of the path were starting to fall over because it just happened that the winds got strong, but at least they stayed up for the ceremony.

Dad and mom, with me and Charlie.

Charlie and I wrote our own vows, and we were married by our family Rabbi, who did the ceremony even though most rabbis at that time did not marry mixed religions [since I was Jewish and Charlie was Presbyterian]. Our religion was music, so we did not care, but it made my family happy that we were married by a rabbi. The ceremony was nice and I was so thinking to myself that I was looking at my partner that I dreamt of since I was young, and never thought this would happen.

Dad & Charlie playing at our wedding, with Aunt Celia in the background.

After the ceremony, music started playing and, even though I felt strange doing so, I danced with my dad. Years later, my sister told me that he thought that my marriage to Charlie would not last.

Our wedding was one of the rare times that my mom and dad were together. We had a lot of family such as my aunts, uncles, cousins and Charlie's mom, dad and sister.

I changed after a while into a long dark green and off-white long dress. Outside waiting for us was a bright lime green Volkswagen Rabbit my father gave us. We were both so excited and happy that we made the choice to finally get married.

As we drove across Alligator Alley, we saw a brush fire that glowed in the dark along the desolate road toward the west coast of Florida. We drove with our dog, Lady, to a lovely motel right on Sanibel Island which is south of Sarasota across from Fort Myers Beach. At that time, the only way to get across to Sanibel was taking a Ferry, but today there is a bridge.

My mother and I getting ready for my wedding to Charlie.

Charlie and I loved Sanibel Island and the Gulf, where you found beautiful calm water and huge conch shells of every type and shape. It was peaceful and a time to relax. Sanibel was also a great memory for me, of when my family would come here to swim and watch the dolphins come close to the shore. You can't express what the sunsets looked like, but they were beautiful. It was a nice time for both of us. After four years of being together, we felt calmness for a little while.

Charlie's parents with us on our wedding day.

MOMENT

By Sheila Dechant

A Moment is felt
You can't buy it, sell it or hold it
The moment goes so quickly

To come from the past to the future
Sometimes my life feels
Like the movements of an orchestra
With each note fits a pattern
Sometimes you know how the song ends
Sometimes you don't
Even the middle of the song can fool
you
It can go somewhere else

Remember the Wizard of Oz?
When Dorothy hit her head and woke up
She saw all the things she cared for
Moving around in the Tornado
As she reached out at that moment
You want to catch it but it goes by so quickly

Hold on to the Moments
Don't look too far
If you always look for tomorrow, you will miss the moment

MARRIED LIFE, MUSIC, AND HALL & OATES

Our lives after we got married pretty much felt the same as before we were married. I did feel more secure in the relationship until something happened that changed everything, including the illusion of security of being in the music world and the business that it is.

Marriage and this lifestyle definitely challenged us when you find that marriage and having a music career is a bad mix. Most of the statistics of relationships with musicians show that they end up in divorce. It's an unstable career more than most other jobs. You pass the talent part, but then you need to make money and still be a viable part of a band, which is tough.

It takes juggling two types of relationships – personal and music/business -- and you have the potential of emotional chaos. You love your spouse; you love the music. You always know that there is someone to take your place both in the band and the marriage.

Tough place to be in for both. Some sacrifice the marriage for the music, and some choose the relationship over the band. The catch is to have someone that understands, and can balance the two. It's not easy, but it does help if you both have a devotion to the arts, which makes a big difference.

I did try to start singing again and even had a successful time singing backup vocal on Joni Mitchell's "Woodstock." When Charlie got a gig playing at Homestead Air Force base, I went up and sang for once and I sounded good, which made me hopeful again. I really enjoyed the large sounding band surrounding me and there was that feeling of floating through the chords and melody. That was really nice for me, but, sadly, it would be a long time before I sang again.

I did get into a band for a very short time with some other girls. The band was Dr. Cool and the Coolettes. You can guess who I was. We worked on some R&B songs but I don't remember what happened. The band disbanded in the end and I think it was because of no financial support. It takes money to make money and music.

Now is the time to hear about the start of a major change in our lives.

Charlie was still playing locally and recording with other bands, including Fantasy and Wolfgang, performing in different clubs around Miami. This was after Buddy Helm, who was fronting the money to financially keep Bethlehem Asylum together, had a record deal, but the band ended up disbanding mostly for financial reasons which happened to many bands in the 70s.

This 60s into the 70s ended the Peace movement. People lived with the philosophy that you can live together on love and peace, but of course they thought pot and drugs would give them that sense of love and togetherness, well-being, and a sense of belonging.

With these ideals came different sex partners, sexually transmitted diseases and then the Vietnam War, with people being drafted. Anger started about the war, which started a lot of protesting. The illusion became a harsh reality and things started to fall apart. The ideas were heartfelt, and then the world as we knew it was never the same.

I was pretty naïve in those days and did not understand why everyone was so into drugs. I did try coke once but I hated it. Pot was okay, but I did not like feeling out of control. I was already a nervous person with anxiety and stomach issues, and that just made it worse.

Charlie did try a little experimenting even before we met, but he has asthma so he did not get into drugs the way most musicians did in those days, and he kept me away from that side of the music world when he could. But you never can get totally away, especially in so many groups that Charlie was in.

One day, Charlie got a call from friends of his who played locally in Miami -- Eddie Zyne, a drummer who later played with The Monkees and other bands, and Stephen Dees, a guitar player and singer who later played with blues Singer Victor Wainwright. Both Steve and Eddie lived in Miami, but they were offered a chance to fly to New York and audition for Daryl Hall and John Oates who had a few hits at that time in the mid-70s, right before Charlie and I were married. Stephen and Eddie got the job and right after Charlie and I were married, Hall and Oates were looking for a sax player. That is when they mentioned Charlie to Daryl.

Charlie and I were still living in the apartment near my sister's house.

Stephen called Charlie to see if he wanted to go up and audition for Daryl and John. Charlie talked to me about it and I said okay, but with hesitation. I said it not knowing what that would entail of him being away, which we rarely were since he played locally or just around Florida.

Charlie went up to New York and he got the job. Well, all of a sudden, I got nervous and did not know what to think about this major change. I was happy for him, but if this would have happened before we were married, this would have been a whole different story. Charlie did ask me if he should take the job. I said no at first, knowing separation would be hard for me, but then he said, "let's give it a year and see what happens."

I knew it would be tough for me more then on him. We loved each other, so it made the decision even harder. Well, I eventually gave in, hoping things would work out for us. I thought of how exciting it would be. This was the big leagues, but still, it was bad timing on a new marriage.

I knew at this point that I would have to give up a lot of things for myself because of the demands of his new job. I made a commitment, so I needed to follow through. You will read a lot of what happened to Charlie because it also affected me as well. I decided to stand by him, but yes, I was torn on what I could accomplish musically. But I realized that he had a better chance of accomplishing something musically when offered this position. Still, I was hoping one day that I could manage to find my way and that I wouldn't feel like I was a burden.

Where Do We Go from Here?

It's been so long
Living in our own closed world
Surrounded by people opening their hearts
It starts opening our world
As we rode back together
The show we played lingers behind
The wall of strangeness comes tumbling down
So sincere
Where do we go from here?
I see the change coming
Looking behind the hidden doors
Yet with fear.
Where do we go from here?

ADJUSTING TO REHEARSALS

The rehearsals in New York began, and our separation from one another started. I was not happy about this transition from us being together to then being apart. I tried to keep busy. My friends, Peggy and Bruce, got me through a lot of times, as did my sister, but I was pretty much alone.

I started to travel with Charlie and got to be in some of the famous recording studios at that time, like the Hit Factory, S.I.R. and Electric Lady recording studios.

When Charlie was home, Peggy and I would go out sometimes but something really strange happened to us.

You the reader won't believe me and you might think I am crazy. I ran into Peggy years later and we both swear to this day that the story I tell you is true.

Peggy and I went out one night to a movie. We both were talking and looking up at the Miami sky as I was driving down 92nd Avenue in South Miami / Kendall area. The sky was bright with lots of stars but very dark where we were on the side streets, heading to the movie theatre. I remember Peggy and I both said at the same time, "Did you see that?" We both saw a spherical shaped object with rounded lights around it. We kept looking at the object. What was really bizarre is the way this strange spherical shape popped up in one place, and the next second it would appear in another part of the sky.

This happened at least three times, moving from one place in the sky and then quickly show up in a different area. We kept saying, "is that a helicopter or plane?" We were getting a little scared, but were fascinated to see this object moving. I kept driving toward it. At one point, it looked so close above us that we started getting very nervous, and turned around and went back home.

Of course, Charlie and Bruce did not believe us. The very next night, the radio station had reported seeing a brightly colored spherical shape about 15 miles from where we saw it the night before, off of the Palmetto Expressway.

We never heard anything else after that, and even now we still believe we saw something that could not be explained.

Charlie continued his rehearsals and the start of his first tour with Hall & Oates began. It seems like he was gone forever. Daryl and john just had some hits out like "Rich Girl," and "Sara Smile," so they were getting pretty popular. One time I went up with Charlie and met everyone. They seemed friendly, but distant. At that time, Tommy Mattolla was the manager for Hall and Oates, and he later became president of Sony Records and married Mariah Cary, which started her career -- but I knew it would end.

I met with Charlie in Manhattan. That was exciting, to be in the music world even though I was not doing any music at that time. I would go with Charlie to some of the recording studios like Electric Lady, where so many greats played, like Jimi Hendrix. I watched the rehearsal and the process of the band together. Or I would go with him to a video shoot, which were the first videos used on the initial start of MTV. I loved watching the process and learned a lot in those days. I was even in one of the video shoots in New York City but I was in a drug store that was being filmed from the outside. I was too shy to come out so no one saw me. The video shoot was done early in the morning, so I was pretty tired.

Seeing it from Charlie's viewpoint, it was all so new and exciting, and to be newlyweds in this single life-style proved to be challenging for both of us. We were in love so that was a plus, even with all the beautiful women surrounding us. I am sure at one point it was very tempting to cheat, but thankfully it never happened for either of us.

The music was so much more important. And, of course, some musicians were playing music to get women, but Charlie did not want to ruin anything musically. And just being newly married while he was just starting, he wanted to do a good job.

I did see lots of women putting themselves in a position to be sexual objects and sexual diseases were probably transmitted, but they didn't seem to care. Getting close to famous performers was all they cared about.

I did see a lot of things going on, but my attitude was that it was none of my business. If musicians wanted to ruin their relationship, that was their choice. I won't mention names, but someone in the management tried to be a little too

Charlie with Daryl Hall.

touchy with me and I got so angry that this person with an important position would act like that, especially to me. One time, I slapped him, and he sure was taken by surprise by my reaction.

One of the times when I was back home, Charlie just got back from a show in Hershey Pennsylvania, they had given the band a huge five-pound Hershey bar. This was so big you would probably go into a diabetic shot.

I was diagnosed with hypoglycemia, and Charlie put the giant chocolate bar way up on our book shelf so that it would be hard for me to reach. He knows I love chocolate. He thought he would outsmart me, but a chocoholic knew there would be a way, especially when he would leave again.

As soon as he left on tour again, I got a chair and got the candy bar down, took a sliver, then wrapped it up and put it exactly where he left it, thinking he would not notice. When he got back, he looked up and half the bar was gone. I gave him an evil smirk and Charlie took it down and threw it away. Well, it was great while it lasted.

The organization had us staying at the Alrae Hotel on East 64th Street. It was a very nice place and close by to Central Park.

While Charlie was rehearsing at S.I.R., I went looking for a dance studio to just exercise and enjoy the art of jazz dancing. I heard about the Alvin Ailey dance studio, so I went over to their location and they told me there were open rehearsal dance classes that I could join. That is what I did. I had the best time.

It was a large dance studio, and what made it special is that they used a band instead of recorded music while you practiced. I really liked learning the choreography in such a professional manner, and it was an honor to be part of Alvin Ailey in such stimulating atmosphere. I knew I could not pursue this as a career because of my spine, but it was still a great experience for me.

If you talk about Alvin Ailey, you have to mention Judith Jamison, who is an American dancer and choreographer. She worked with Agnes DeMille for the American Ballet Theatre and then was asked to join Alvin Ailey Dance theatre. She did some other ballet projects, but came back to Alvin Ailey, where she was known for one of the noted dances, "Revelation."

I did not just sit and watch the Hall and Oates rehearsals because I was particularly interested in the process of how the show was created. The environment is very businesslike, but relaxed. Daryl mainly would take the lead on what the arrangements should sound like. The band finding its own way to interpret what Daryl needed and how to put everything together to get the sound he wanted, with John following his lead and putting in his own ideas. Each band member was working hard to get as close to what Daryl wanted to hear. It is a long creative process, but in the end, the music evolves and everyone starts feeling more comfortable. I enjoyed watching the process and definitely wished that I could eventually work on my music.

I found myself not just being married to a musician, but I definitely turned out to be a different kind of wife. I always felt that I am me first. I hated being labeled, "the wife." I was trying to make a unique situation that loved Charlie, and I wanted to learn as much as I could. I think that is when I started trying to compose my own songs more seriously while making sure the marriage stayed strong.

Charlie was very easy going and seemed content at this point. His laid-back attitude of "I love you, and we are together, and I want to play music and that's that." I, on the other hand, felt like an unwelcome guest for a long time. I knew that Charlie wanted me there, yet was a little confused, since he was starting his musical career and a new marriage too.

I said to myself, "stay strong." However, it sometimes made me sad that we all love the same thing and that kindness and understanding would have made quite a difference in many of these organizations. For many, it's all about self-expression, self-preservation and big egos.

Meeting Daryl and John was very uncomfortable to me and I felt shy around them. I thought Daryl was very distant. It was the first time I met someone who was not very friendly, but cordial. Charlie said it could have been that he was shy, too, so I needed to take that into consideration. He kept his feelings quite hidden, and coming from a lot of friendly relaxed musicians my whole life, I was surprised by that kind of distant vibe.

Over the past 40- plus years, Daryl pretty much stayed separated from any relationships within the band or their families, but once in a while when he is relaxed and confident, out of nowhere he would say with a smile that caught me by surprise, "hello, Sheila." I would reply, "how are you doing, Daryl?" and I think he was taken a back, like no one ever asked him how he was.

I always thought John was a very nice person and in the early days, I figured that all musicians were out for getting women, which they sometimes did. However, John always seemed to be looking for that special person and seemed more down to earth. I liked that. I think that, for a long-time, people did not pay enough attention to him, and I am so glad that he has stepped out of the shadows and showed his talent more. Years later, he did find a special person, Aimee, who has been with him ever since.

Aimee and I have known each other off and on over the years and I guess you could say we are distant friends. We don't live near each other, but once in a while we will connect via email or phone.

This job was about loving to play music, but in my opinion, the business behind the creating of songs is a necessary evil if bands are going to succeed. You can't have one without the other. But the business part needs to stay as far away as possible while the creative process continues.

I guess for some performers it doesn't bother them, but when I am some-times there and the management comes in, the atmosphere does change. I understand that you have to make money, but in the early 70s, there were a lot of musicians that lost a lot of money with a lot of wheeling and dealing with the record companies. There were companies that had so much financial control that a lot of musicians lost so much money because they were taken advantage of. Musicians were given misguided information. The so-called financial advisors took more then what a performer made. The musicians were so naïve about the way the business people were selling their songs. They were losing the rights to their music and making the businessmen wealthy, while they were struggling.

Percentage of sales of records and shows went to the management. The advances given to the bands were paid back, but they still lost profit from the corporations, taking more then they should have.

The performers' lack of knowledge, never questioning how they were getting paid and where the money came from, was some of the reasons they ended up losing their money. If management was honest and would have explained things to them but, they didn't do that, so that they could profit.

I did see a lot of money being spent during that time, but the band was given a weekly salary. They were surrounded by the wealthy, but never made much money. The back-up players hadn't a clue on how they were being paid, but they could not say anything. You can't rock the boat or you could be out of a job. Charlie and I always felt we were surrounded by the wealthy, and we were so close, yet so far away, from being financially comfortable. I also realized that Charlie's talent and my understanding, we managed to stay afloat when so many careers had ended.

Over the years, we have met so many talented musicians and how bad we both felt that so many still struggle yet persevere to show their abilities and amazing creativity, still not to be recognized or accepted within their own peers. It is so unfair to me, but it is the nature of the business and truthfully, luck. I feel the industry overlooked and let the world see their talent but, I especially admire so many of them today.

Years later, I understood that most musicians backing up the main lead performers were the employees and the main acts were the employers. I know some bands like Bruce Springsteen and the E Street Band were separated financially like a mini corporation, so that the E Street Band could reap some of the benefits with Bruce over the years, so they made out well. I just wished this was explained to the back-up musicians playing behind the main acts. Playing music, and the glamorous lifestyle they were surrounded with, ended a lot of careers in the long run. As wonderful as it was for the main performers in most bands, it was a constant financial struggle for the backup bands and band members.

I can't make excuses for this financial burden -- unless you're a musician that takes control of his or her finances and either becomes a leader in the band or save as much as you can. Some musicians did get out front, but some did not want to take that responsibility or want to be in control of their own band. The main performers had managers to help them, while the back-up musician was basically on their own. Having the attitude that I should just play and have fun is great until you are bankrupt or out of a job.

My goodness, I never knew -- and probably no one else did -- that playing music could be so complicated. That is the sad part of trying to love something you want to do and seeing the hardship that so many endured over the years.

Daryl and John were some of the lucky few that lost everything and finally got control of their finances and creative ideas. They came back stronger than ever. I do admire what they did. The wonderful ideas that Daryl had about starting an internet show became very successful. Charlie got to play on some of them over the years.

I knew that just the members of the band were family and everyone else was an outsider. It was an uncomfortable position to be in, when you're in a relationship with a band member and how it affects home life and trying to start a family, but still be close to music. I saw a lot of marriages being destroyed for that reason. I was lucky in that respect with my background, since childhood. I understood the many aspects of playing music, working and raising a family. Some well-known entertainers accepted and welcomed band members and their families, although it did cause a lot of separations and long touring dates. Some families would come on the road once in a while. But it was more difficult for the back-up band with their spouses and children to come because of financial issues; basically, they couldn't afford it.

I have seen a lot of musicians leave for some reason or another, mostly getting offered better paying jobs or deciding to quit touring because of separation from their family. I have seen management change over and over again. I guess Charlie and I are rare in that we understood the nature of this life-style and its ups and downs, knowing we would have to make sacrifices for the art in so many ways.

Because of Charlie and my love for music and him, I did feel like I was "The Outside Looking In." Blending off and on with the musicians and feeling very comfortable, listening to their music ventures. I seem to be accepted, which was nice, and I never over-stepped my bounds, and knew when to stand back. Seeing how the fans interact, celebrities, money being needed for equipment, lighting, stage set up, tour staff, merchandizing, catering, ticket sales, and how the sound throughout the venue was set up. The amazing crew who work so hard -- they are the back bone of keeping the tour together.

Management came in once in a while to see how everything is going, but I always feel a little tension when they come or it's just me.

I was in a strange position when on the road, but what an adventure it has been. I occasionally get bored, mostly because I am not participating, but that was okay. I always find something to do. I understand the musical interaction that happens between band members on stage. It's just like being on a football team. There is inside-musical language, which I sometimes tune into when I am on the side of the stage.

I remember standing on the side for years watching all the fans try to get as close as possible. I never understood why they do that, but Charlie said it's to feel the vibe from the stage. I just don't think you need to be right up to a performer's feet or try to grab them to feel the music. Like I said, I was never celebrity crazy.

I remember, I was about 28 at the time, and on the road with Charlie and the band. After a show, we went back to our New York hotel, and all of a sudden, these girls came running in, looking for Daryl, John, and/or the rest of the band. Charlie had me by the hand, walking toward the elevator, when these fans started running toward him. He pulled me into the elevator and I turned to him and said, "I want to watch this!" Charlie didn't want to have anything to do with that situation. He was pretty shy, and his social skills were not that great. He did get a little better over the years with practice. It was fun watching that, though. Charlie sometimes reminded me of the same characteristics that Daryl had, with a stand-off-ish attitude sometimes. Over the years, as time went by, they both got better at being more sociable.

Of course, when you are the crew and start feeling things getting a little tedious doing tours day after day, you have to spice it up just a little. One time, while Daryl and John didn't know it, one of the guys from the band would throw guitar picks at us, usually at the end of the tour, and of course we would reciprocate, but it was done quickly without anybody knowing to make things fun. We would laugh about it. I guess the crew accepted me, which was nice and made being on the road comfortable most times. Acceptance is very important for the long haul and daily routine of the job.

You may get some clarity when I point out that it is the Hall and Oates and the back-up band. Yes, Charlie has a fan base and gets major solos throughout the show, but he is the not the main draw as you must know. He was still an employee. You have to be careful, because at any time you could be let go -- yes, even him. So you had to know how to talk without causing any drama, which Charlie did very well. His talent was always there, but also the way he worked with the performers is a great asset.

But for me, I saw so many unfair practices within the company, and could not understand why we were still struggling financially. I also understand that, like any business, if you don't own it, you're at the mercy of the main performers and management. Again, surrounded by the rich and famous.

I remember one time Charlie played at Madison Square Garden, and the audience reaction to his main solo was amazing. He was given a standing ovation that roared through the whole arena. I think that strengthened his place in the band, or so we thought -- until Charlie was fired.

Yes, you read that right. At one point in 1978, they let him go right before we found out that I was pregnant. Charlie was doing so well that we decided to start a family.

In retrospect, Charlie was caught between family plus an unstable job you love. I, on the other hand, was caught between having a strong marriage, adjust to this organization and making sure of my own identity, my talents and that I was strong enough to deal with this lifestyle. As you can see now, this is not easy.

What makes the creating process is the people you love and the people you connect to that brings inspiration to the work. If they had that philosophy, life on the road would be nicer and relationships would be stronger. If you just want to connect to other musicians then were does family come in?

Family starts feeling like they are outsiders of your life. Bingo! You divorce and you wonder why. I also feel if you want it that way, then don't get married to a musician. It is hurtful to the people who love you. You can be self-centered all you want, but at one point, you will lose for shutting out feelings for others in the long run.

Sometimes, when performers are on stage, they play like this is a job and I can feel that. Other times you can tell when the emotions for the songs are there and mean something to everyone around you playing.

If your loved one is there to support you, that feeling should transcend to them, as well. You can not only sense it, but see it in their eyes. Now, that is what I call "playing music with heart and soul." I wonder if musicians forget that sometimes. Music comes from the heart and not just notes. It goes deeper than that. Does it always have to be about something bad happening in a relationship? Does becoming a professional mean losing those you love? I do agree that significant others need their own life to feel valuable, but when you don't have people clapping for your accomplishments, does that make the person less important?

I also got a great understanding of Charlie's role and being married in this kind of environment. It is like being with someone in the military. Leaving for long periods of time and then coming back. I call this "an emotional roller coaster." I did get used to that way of life, and it allowed me to concentrate on my interests, but I soon realized this would be a forever career for Charlie, which affected the children and me. That was something I had to have a serious thought about... should I still commit? I didn't know what was ahead of me when Charlie took this role in the band.

THE ROCK STAR

By Sheila DeChant

I can't touch you
You're way above the crowd
Your sound carries through souls
Through all the people below you
He's a Rock Star

Camouflage his past he can't
What makes up look up?
To make him so large
The people below his voice
Wonder in fascination
Who Is this Rock Star?

When he steps down
From the stage
The sound lingers on
As you walk back to the car

While backstage the thoughts of what went on
Remain unspoken
The left-over energy is still there
Coming down from the high
Until the next time
When the music, the crowd
Emotions
Come back again and again

VIEW FROM BELOW

By Sheila DeChant
I can't touch you
You're way above the crowd
Your voice carries
Sends you feeling through all souls
Who's this Singer of Songs?

Camouflage his past he can
Yet, he makes up look up with that sound
He looks so large from below
The people hear the voice
Wonder in fascination
Who is this person?

Catching some of the words
Relate to the feelings
Beautiful sound
I hope it never ends
Continues on long after their gone from the stage.

The Sound continues for hours
Each chord surrounds us
I wonder what they are thinking
Looking down at the masses.

The following pages are directly from my Journal I started in 1979. It gives you an idea of what it was like being in this lifestyle, especially after they let Charlie go in 1978.

January 13, 1979

We spent the night at Dad's, then after a fun hour of repacking the car... we said so long to Florida, not knowing what was ahead of us. Before we left, Charlie and I decided to start a family.

I was really surprised to see my dad so upset before we left. I think that was the first time that I saw him show any emotion toward me. I started feeling sad, too. Charlie and I were just feeling weird, but glad the trip was starting. I drove first all the way to Wildwood, Florida, stopping to give Lady a break, dog exercising, bathroom and then terrible roadside food.

The full moon was out and at the beginning of the Turnpike we listened to Steve Martin's new comedy record. Charlie and I told each other about the books we were reading. I also took a picture of a fake dummy with a space-suit which was at the first gas station stop.

I got a little nauseous for some reason, but I figured it was from nerves and not serious.

We reached Tallahassee around 10:15 p.m. and took a long time to find a motel.

Boy! We were so tired and crabby, but this was the last of the boring Florida Turnpike. I shouted some fond remarks and a few bird signs at finally leaving the dreaded road.

Lady, my sweet Border Collie, looked like she was in utter misery in the car, but I hope she gets better over time.

January 14, 1979

We ate breakfast next door at Howard Johnson's restaurant and I love their clam strips. We decided to switch the driving every two hours. We pulled off for gas in a small town in Florida and took a picture of a gigantic house, which was bright yellow. Then got back onto Route 10 toward Mobile, Alabama, where we stopped at Ocean Springs for dinner. We were getting tired but we ate fried chicken, which turned out to be really good. I bought some postcards, but there were not a lot of sights to see except the Mississippi River and the Gulf. We listened to Joni Mitchell, Steely Dan and some Jazz.

Finally, after nine hours of driving, we reached New Orleans around 8 p.m. We did get lost, as usual, finding the motel and had to cross the river on route 90 to the other side, but finally found the Travel Lodge that we booked. The rooms were not bad with a King size bed. We zonked out early as we watched an old movie called, "Daddy Long Legs," starring Fred Astaire.

I call Dad and he told me how hot it was back home.

This also was when I realized I had not gotten my period in 14 days but I just thought it was stress.

We got up at 9 a.m. and went to the famous Café Du Monde for coffee and these deep-fried fattening delicious powdered warm pastries. Then we went looking for gifts in the stores and Charlie got a Jazz T-shirt. I looked at beautiful dolls, then we stopped in a restaurant and had sausage and chili. What a combination that was.

We headed back and got Lady from the car and headed toward Bourbon Street. We kept running into this musician who self-made all of these rhythm instruments.

Bourbon Street was very interesting and I bought a red Jazz T-shirt and saw one lady in pasties, dancing inside a bar as we walked by. The funny articles we saw in the store windows like ball warmers and pasties. I thought how ridiculous but fun to see all the crazy items.

We headed back to the motel around 4:30 p.m. and as usual we got lost finding the motel.

We went to eat at this restaurant not on Bourbon street called, "Tchoupi-toulas Planation," which was once owned by a madam. We drove across a bridge and you had to look hard to find the place. It doesn't look like a restaurant but was built like an Acadian styled home. The front part of the house is 220 years old and it was known as a house of prostitution and is now used for having dinners and weddings. Tchoupitoulas is an Indian name that means mighty river and it was the home of the famous madam, Norma Wallace, who for decades was the most celebrated bordello madam in New Orleans. The waiter said she was quite a woman in those days. She sold the place n 1968. We were told that after she passed away that sometimes you can see her ghost walking down the stairs. We really liked the atmosphere of the place and so much history.

January 16, 1979

Not much happened this day. We just did a lot of driving to Houston and passed by Baton Rouge and Lafayette.

It was pretty hazy and foggy weather, surrounded by miles and miles of trees as we went over the Ponchartrain Lake. We stopped at the Welcome building at the border of Texas.

Our hotel was the Ramada Inn and it was near the Astrodome. I watched the movie, "Funny Lady," with Barbara Streisand and part of "Shampoo" starring Warren Beatty, while Charlie read his book. For dinner, we ate at a place called, "Victorian Station," and had Prime Rib and steak. The food was excellent but the waiters were really slow.

We turned in for the night pretty early as we were headed to Austin, Texas to see Charlie's Uncle Bernie and wife Laverne.

January 17, 1979

The road to Austin was long but nice. It was our first trip on empty roads and up and down hills. It was raining pretty badly until we got to Ozona, Texas when we started having car trouble with the carburetor again, but we thought it was from the rain. We stopped at a gas station and it turned out the hose was torn so we got it replaced. The rest of the ride was quiet and peaceful. We only got a little lost finding Bernie and Laverne's house, but we made it.

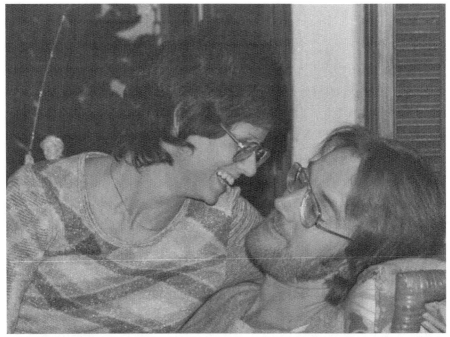

Laverne met me and Charlie at the door. She's really pretty with reddish hair and that wonderful Texan accent that I was not used to. We all had coffee and talked. Laverne and I had found something in common: headaches. I really liked her a lot. Her bubbly personality made us all smile and made it a great evening. Our dog, Lady, and Laverne's miniature Doberman pincher got along. Laverne told us about the job she had and the guy who fired her and what a slob he was. I went and took a shower while Charlie and Laverne got dog food for Lady. Bernie came home around 5 p.m. He works for the phone company and so does his son, Lindsey. Laverne also worked at the phone company.

We all ate at a Mexican restaurant, including Lindsey's wife, Brenda. Mexican food is known in Texas and it definitely was great.

We mostly talked about music and jobs. We came back to the house and the conversations continued until 11 p.m. but with traveling all day we were exhausted and headed for bed. We called Charlie's mom and gave my dad a signal call. [If you don't understand a signal call, in those days to save on a phone bill, you quickly call and basically say we are okay and hang up before the phone company charges you for the call.]

We got up at 8 a.m. I wasn't feeling so good. My stomach felt bad, so I was guessing it was the Mexican food from the night before.

Laverne made us waffles and Charlie had an egg. Laverne felt better after the bad headache she had last night. We talked for a while, then we packed. We had a great time with them and I felt bad that we had to leave. I will always remember their kindness and making me feel comfortable. [A side note: Laverne passed away October 7, 2016 at age 93 of heart and kidney failure, and Bernie passed away February 21, 2009 at the age of 92.]

As usual we got lost again getting out of Austin, but we made it out for the next 200-mile drive to Carlsbad, New Mexico. I drove the first 100 miles and Charlie drove the rest of the way. I wasn't feeling too good, but we made good time. We even stopped for a quick pee on the side of the road. That must have been quite a sight, with me stooping beside the car. Lady must have loved watching us. We got into Carlsbad around 7:30 p.m. and of course we got lost, but finally found the motel. The two heavy set girls at the desk were not very pleasant and half the night the heater didn't work. We were both exhausted, so Charlie got some food and brought back to the room. I took a bath, which helped, and we fell asleep quickly.

January 19, 1979

What an interesting morning this was, I had a feeling that something was wrong with me. It must have been after Texas that nausea hit me so bad. We got more Saltine Crackers and then I decided to get the pregnancy test but decided to wait till we got too Carlsbad. Thank goodness for the Saltine Crackers, which did help me get through the car ride.

The next morning, I finally did the pregnancy test and, sure enough, it was positive. We looked at each other and Charlie gave me a quick smile and said, "let's go to the Caverns!" and that was that. We pretty much knew it was going to be positive and we were not surprised, but that didn't stop us from seeing the famous Caverns we heard about. It was our way of celebrating.

We went into the Caverns. At first it was so dark and spooky, but we got used to it. As our eyes adjusted, we saw how beautiful the place was. We admired all the colors as we continued walking down the hill for almost two miles. We then had ham sandwiches and a candy bar for lunch. Charlie wanted to go to the part of the cavern called "The Big Rooms," which was another mile or more, but I was getting tired. I just found out I was pregnant, celebrating in a cavern plus walking almost four miles or so. Any ways, we did it. It was so beautiful that it was worth the extra walking. Luckily, the cavern had an elevator that took us up to the gift shop where I got postcards and a few horse place mats, and Charlie got a bat charm.

The next day, we continued our journey through the Guadalupe Mountains, which put us back into Western Texas. It was also a beautiful drive. We got into the Caballero Motel and the room was much nicer than the one in Carlsbad. Of course, when you are in this area, you have to eat Mexican food, which we ordered in the room. Boy! Charlie over-did the eating and I thought he was either pregnant or was going to burst into the Mexican hat dance. I just had the chicken, which was pretty bad.

Charlie went outside of the motel and did laundry. At this time of year, it was really cold but he wanted to get it over with.

January 31, 1979

We got to Los Angeles and found this low budget motel efficiency near Universal Studios, and I did not like the place at all. A lot of strange characters were staying there, but finally Charlie found a nice apartment that was owned by a lawyer and real close to Universal.

I went to my first doctor's appointment and it was a disaster. The nurse was very condescending and told me the test I took was bad, and she said to stay out of her way while she tested the urine. I think she was just trying to get more money out of my visit.

The office seemed unorganized. The doctor walked in and examined me while talking about what to eat. The information I got from him was very vague, but he said I was about seven weeks and, "see ya," he said, and walked out. He wouldn't tell me the cost, but it was his cold attitude toward my first pregnancy exam. This was not enjoyable at all. How sad.

So, here I am with Charlie in an apartment in Los Angeles. We came here because he thought his friend, Buddy, could help him find some work. It was so difficult for us not knowing why Hall and Oates let him go, and just when we decided to start a family. Great timing!! We were so happy about the baby, but this was bittersweet.

Charlie would go off with Buddy, while I stayed at the apartment. I was starting to get stir crazy and I did not have a car. I was becoming increasingly unhappy and Charlie did not find any work.

Then, out of the blue, after being in Los Angeles a month, Charlie got a call from the Hall and Oates manager, Tommy Mattolla, who offered his job back if we moved to New York. It seems they offered the sax job to a well-known player, Lenny Pickett, who now plays on Saturday Night Live. Lenny turned down the offer, but recommended that Hall and Oates reach out to, guess who? That's right, the one and only Charlie DeChant. And so they went back to Charlie. I guess it was either fate or luck, who knows?

But Tommy said that we would have to move to New York since that is where all the rehearsals are. So here we go again.

MOVING ON

By Sheila Dechant
Moving On it's time to go
Another stage
More secret doors to go through
Moving on, it's time to go

My dreams so splendid
Riding a horse to the ocean
Not looking back but forward
Heading right toward it
Just moving on, moving on

It's strange, unknown
We can't see what's ahead

Souls and sounds be our guide
Jut moving on, moving on

The Hall and Oates organization hired someone to drive our car to New York from Los Angeles and paid for our flight to New York City, where I mentioned previously was the Alrae Hotel. This was our home base for a while as Charlie rehearsed for the next tour.

After a while, someone from the management office took us around to some apartments outside Manhattan. I had some relatives on Long Island, so we looked in Queens, which was not as expensive as living in the city. Some of the apartments we saw were pretty bad, but one of the last ones we looked at was nice, and later we found out it was owned by Donald Trump's dad.

Our apartment was very big with two bedrooms. As you walk in from the front door into a hall, on the right was the kitchen, and as you continued on into a huge living room with the large window facing the front of the building so you can see who was coming or going. As you continue on to the back, there were two bedroom and the bathroom in the middle, and also a door that leads to the back door where the yard was the top of the garage and a small grass area to the left where yellow daisies grew in the spring time. Next to the backdoor was the neighbor's back door, but if you wanted to visit them at their front door you had to go to the elevator and cross over to the other side of the building and take another elevator up to their apartment. There was a security doorman that had a podium near the front door of the apartment.

Very strange, I thought, especially having lived in Miami most of my life. It was so strange to me that I felt very uncomfortable, but I knew I had to get used to my new environment since Charlie was going on tour soon.

Parking was an issue unless you could afford a parking space in the garage. When you park in the streets you had to move your car at certain times or it would be towed.

Two long blocks from the apartment was the subway train E or F that you can take into the city with stops like Forest Hills or the Queens Plaza Mall.

I met my next-door neighbors, Donna and Todd, so that was good. I finally met someone but mainly focused on the getting the room ready for the baby and visiting the doctor for check-ups.

I must admit, I had a great pregnancy. My hair was thick and my nails were strong, and up to the last few months I felt pretty good.

Very soon after we moved in, Charlie left for the four-to-six-week tour. The hardest part is the leaving. I was in a strange city and I really had no choice, but it did make me sad. He would write me lots of letters, mostly telling me about the places he was and the shows he played or any problems that happened on stage or problems with his horn. I really didn't want too hear about the places, since I wasn't there, but I listened anyways. Eventually, he would send me the tour itinerary so I would know where he was at. Years later, traveling with Charlie, I got to know a lot of places also, so when Charlie tells me now, I can picture where he is at and imagine what I would do if I was there. There were times I was just glad I wasn't there. Traveling can be very exhausting sometimes, but it has it's perks too.

Loneliness creeps in at strange times of the day, but I try not to think about it. I started writing stories and lyrics, which I loved to do because I can say whatever I want without anyone judging me. Composing music again kept me busy but my mind was on the baby. I was alone and pregnant and I tried to cope with the situation the best I could. Meeting Donna, Todd and their children helped a little.

I went for medical check-ups by taking the train. I had to figure out which train to take and what stop. The Queens Plaza mall was only 3 stops and you would go up stairs that seemed to last forever but the mall was right there. Around my seventh month, the stairs were getting harder for me to climb.

I really felt like I was on another planet compared to Florida. I felt alienated but hopeful that things would get better.

Music kept on moving farther and farther away from me. I had hopes to eventually have it a part of my life again, but the only link I had was Charlie.

September 17, 1979

I was due soon and Charlie's sister, Janine, came up from Florida to be there for us, and she is also a nurse. She and Charlie started building a bookshelf in the living room.

It seems everyone was making suggestions how to get me to go into labor, but I was afraid to try anything at this point. I decided on a natural birth, and just wanted the baby to come.

We all decided to take the Subway train to Manhattan to eat at our favorite restaurant, Mama Leones. If I haven't told you, Charlie can sleep anywhere sitting, standing, eating, reading. I wish I could do that. While we were heading into Manhattan, Charlie had to stand but luckily, I got a seat. About 10 minutes into the trip I look up and Charlie is holding on to the pole, sound asleep. See, he has other talents too. Ha!

The restaurant opened a half century ago in 1906 until about 1994 in the theatre district on 44th street between Broadway and 8th Avenue near the Majestic Theater. I even found an original recipe:

Mama Leones's Eggs with Zucchini

1	small zucchini
2	1 tablespoon olive oil
3	2 Tablespoons butter or margarine
4	Four fresh eggs
5	2 slices mortadella, salami or prosciutto, diced
6	Dash of salt and pepper

Peel the zucchini and cut into thin slices. Heat olive oil and butter in skillet. Add zucchini and cover for 5 minutes.

Add meat and cover for another 5 minutes. Add eggs, cover and cook for 4 minutes or until set. Sprinkle cheese on top

Serves 2

September 19, 1979

I am now nine months pregnant and due anytime. It's been a few tough months since we left California. We went back to Miami for a couple of weeks, then made the final move and decision to relocate to New York. Charlie is on a loan of $15,000 from Daryl and John, but it has not been a happy time financially ... always struggling to pay bills, even while working for a famous group. Some weeks would go by without the call to go on the road again, and Charlie would start collecting unemployment to help us through.

We started Lamaze classes together. It has been a good shared experience, but it was also a lot of strain not knowing what was going to happen to us. I am looking forward to having the baby, but I was worried about the loneliness and boredom, especially when Charlie goes back on tour -- which we found out would be in October.

There were some strange times, later in my pregnancy, when I would go with Charlie to some shows especially in Manhattan.

I remembered one time after a show, we went to this club and I am sitting at a table when I was about seven months along and all the sexy women were around me, throughout the club. I guess it was the big time, but I am definitely big and feeling out of place. This famous model came over to Charlie and was sitting right next to me like I wasn't there. Really!! You couldn't miss me. Anyway's, she was really flirty and saying how wonderful Charlie was. I did not know whether to hit her or get up and go home. I just sat there feeling foolish and out of place, but Charlie wanted me to come.

Groupies did not bother me, but when you're this pregnant, your emotions are all over the place. I felt farther and farther away from the music and it was not a good feeling. The good thing was Charlie didn't seem interested, but if I was in that situation, I would be tempted. If he was, he hid his feelings well.

September 24, 1979

Finally, on September 24th, while Janine and Charlie were still working on the bookshelf, I went into the bathroom and neatly, without a mess, my water broke. I walked into the living room and told them my water broke. You should have seen their look of disbelief. So many false alarms and two weeks overdue, but this was for real.

At first, the labor pains felt like pressure, and I kept thinking too myself that this wasn't too bad.

Literally, 35 hours of emotions, exhaustion, pain and struggling, but I must admit the Lamaze helped me with the waves of pain.

In those days, no pain medication was recommended because it could harm the baby. I remember holding Charlie's hand so tight to get through the pain. I did pretty well, considering no medicine. I did remember not to fight the pain as it went through waves, and then calm before the storm again, but I pictured the baby being helped out with each wave with rhythm of the contractions and it was working with the elements inside. Don't laugh, but it was like two musicians connecting musically -- but I was connecting with Jennifer instead, and there she was, with bright blue eyes like the sky and silver hair that later turned blonde. Luckily, Charlie was there, and seeing him with tears in his eyes was so touching that I forgot about the pain.

My dad with Jennifer.

She was our first child and we were both excited and scared, not knowing what having a baby would be like. We were so lucky that she turned out to be a good baby, and you felt the sweetness in her soul from the day she was born. I had mixed feelings about her. Your body doesn't feel right, so trying to re-cuperate and focusing on my daughter was hard emotionally. I went through a roller coaster of feelings. She was mine and looking down at her, you just can't believe this little girl came out of me. Her little hands and feet were so small, and I remember putting her little foot into the palm of my hand. I had never seen those bright eyes so blue before.

The nurses were so wonderful, and we couldn't wait for the time we could bring her home, and you don't realize that your world, as you know it, has changed forever.

Something, though, was happening to Jennifer.

It was quite scary when they said she had jaundice and they put her in this incubator with her little eyes covered. I felt so helpless, seeing her lying there all alone. It made me sad. We had too leave her there for a few days, so talk about torturing the parents and you'd think that it would be great to get the extra sleep. Nope, didn't sleep, just worried.

I remember lying in the hospital bed , Jennifer would look at me and, no kidding, she was smiling at me and I know it was not gas because when we went to the elevator to take her home, she was looking at the nurse and all of a sudden, she started smiling at her, too. Even the nurse commented that she is smiling right at me. She definitely was a happy baby.

Well, the journey of bringing home a baby started and we were nervous with sleepless nights ahead, making sure she was breathing, getting over my body going through the changes of giving birth.

I remember being scared at first when I had to give her a bath for the first time, and taking her little outfit off and washing this tiny little baby. Wrapping her and seeing this fragile baby, and you had to somehow bond with her, and the feelings happened quickly. I think every Mom goes through the "what to do" phase and so worried you would hurt the baby. No matter how much you prepare, even going through all the nurse's directions at the hospital didn't seem to make me feel adequate enough to take care of her. It was not easy to adjust at first with sleepless nights that didn't help, yet those eyes just stared at me and, with that trusting look, my life changed forever.

I did become possessive of anyone holding Jennifer, including Charlie. This was the first time my protective instincts kicked in. Staring at her, day in and day out, whether she was asleep or not. Truthfully, I was a mess.

September 7, 1980

I just got through reading this book to Charlie. It was great to start reading again.

You can't relax too much with a baby, but slowly we got into a good rhythm that seemed to work. Jennifer is now eleven months old. It's been a real rough year for me. I didn't think Charlie and I were going to stay together. I felt really tired from the birth, even after all these months, I just felt something was wrong with me.

I walked into Jennifer's room to pick her up and I was so weak, I couldn't lift her. I knew something was not right. I was weak, tired, gaining weight instead of going back to my regular weight of 112. Then my hair started falling out. Finally, it was time to see a doctor.

I had lab tests done and found out I had hypothyroidism. I was so lucky that Jennifer was a good baby, so it helped me as I was trying to get better. Years later, I saw another doctor and had more labs done and he asked me if I ever had cancer. I promptly answered no, but very concerned when he said that. The reason was my thyroid had shrunk to peas, which could be a side-effect of chemotherapy. My own immune system was attacking my thyroid glands. This is known as Hashimoto Disease. It took a long time to figure out a dosage for me that would work. After being on the medication for a while, my weight still climbed in a matter of weeks and, to this day, I still fight the weight with some good days and then bad days. I never let it get the best of me, so, as much as I could, I placed all my energy in Jennifer, music and dance when I could find time.

I did not have any family close by and with Charlie coming and going it didn't make life so easy, but I really loved watching Jennifer grow.

Jennifer continued to show her sweetness, like snapping her fingers at four months old, or when Charlie would blow his nose really hard, Jennifer would jump from the sound. Later, when she first started to speak, she looked down at her belly button and then looked up at me and said, "dada?" You had to be there.

September 8, 1980

The next day, the heartfelt goodbyes again because Charlie was leaving for a six-week tour of Europe, Japan, Australia and New Zealand. We just couldn't afford for me to go, and with a baby in tow, I don't think Daryl would have had much patience with us.

I didn't feel safe in the neighborhood, and the government changed the zone to where the low-income families with government subsidies moved to our area. I decided to pay extra and get a car space in our garage, as I got tired of moving my car from one side of the street to the other. The garage space helped a lot. I am so glad I decided to get a space.

My friend, Christine, came to spend a couple of days with us. She was a flight attendant and had some time to see me. It was so great to see her. I was glad for the company, but it was a short visit.

Not easy for me with this long stretch of touring. Sadness comes and goes, but we needed the money. The long distance calls from Charlie helped a lot, and this was our only option, since we did not have family that lived close by.

I started exercise classes and I met a girl named Ruth, and went to her house, where I met her husband Stephen, who was a composer. They were much younger than I was, but were very nice. I wrote some lyrics for some music he wrote, but we both didn't like the song, so he said we would try it again later. I didn't like being away from Jennifer for more than an hour, so never had time to change and complete the song.

So here I am with a two-year old, alone in Queens and Charlie on tour. I didn't have any plans except to live day-by-day and see where it would take me. I decided that I would start dance classes somewhere to get some exercise, as I did love to dance too.

I found a dance studio called Showtime Dance Studio, and it was run by a Broadway dancer. His name was Gary Gendall, but first I had to find a babysitter. I went to one class when Charlie came home and the mother of the dance school recommended a girl name Nicole, who had babysat other children. So I decided to give her a try.

The classes started and I mainly focused on jazz dancing. I really enjoyed it, and we did a couple of shows for the studio, and one of the stage productions was Michael Jackson's "Thriller." That was my last show, when I noticed something wrong with Jennifer and I could not figure out what it was.

Jennifer was always close to me, but became unusually clingy every time I went to the door to leave. She was two-years-old and it was getting harder for me to leave her, but I knew I needed some kind of outlet and Nicole was my way to take a break. Besides, it was only a one-hour jazz class.

One day, I came back and, after Nicole left, I diapered Jennifer, looked down at her buttocks, and they were all black and blue welts. I was so taken aback and upset, as you can imagine. Jennifer was also very congested, so I took her to the pediatrician. He said it could be a virus, but if I wanted, to take her to the hospital to run some tests. I headed right to the hospital.

I would definitely say this was one of the worst experiences of my life. The nurse took her to a room and they told me that it looked like Jennifer was being abused. The shocker came when they asked my two-year-old with limited vocabulary who hurt you, she said, "Mommy." Meaning she wanted me to hold her, but they twisted her words to mean something else. She was asking for me, but the next thing I knew, they took her from me. I felt pain and a sickness in my stomach.

I followed social services in another car, to where they took Jennifer to -- Queens Hospital -- and was put in a crib with high railings. I was so exhausted that when Jennifer went to sleep, I went home to try and sleep, too. I realized the only one that could have done this to her was Nicole. I called her mother, who yelled at me for accusing her daughter. I just knew she had done it, but how to prove it was going to be tough, with no witnesses.

I called Charlie and there was a discussion with management to get involved, but I didn't feel this was right. Years later, I regretted that I may have made the wrong choice on them helping.

I would visit Jennifer every day and stay with her as long as I could until, finally, I was allowed to take her home.

Later, a social worker came to the apartment and saw that I had a nice home for Jennifer. The only thing I was sad about was Jennifer's favorite blanket was still at the hospital,1 but I couldn't go back there.

Finally, some answers about what happened to Jennifer came to light. The mother of the dance school told me that Nicole's older sitter had put a baby in hot water. Why would the school recommend her sister? I was so hurt and frustrated. We did not have much money, and to put Jennifer through the courts again at this young age would not have helped the situation. The whole case with social services was dropped, and the final verdict ended up being my word against Nicole.

I never went back to the dance school again.

Sometime in 1981

My nightmares and depression started and I never left Jennifer again. This kind of trauma never leaves you, even to this day but thank God she never showed any signs of emotional scars

Later, when Jennifer was older, she told me that Nicole got mad at her and started hitting her with a toy hammer. Made me sick thinking this was happening to my daughter.

Me with my friend of 40 years, Grace.

The stress of Charlie not being here for me was intense. I became pregnant again, but then I miscarried. I was alone and dealt with this the best I knew how. I had to pick myself up, and decided I have to meet some people or I will go crazy. The thought of leaving Charlie was a possibility but I kept saying to myself, "it will get better, I hope." I know Charlie was trying to take care of us and, being a side man, I also knew the organization didn't care. Business is business. You do the job or you're fired. That was scary for both of us.

Charlie liked his job, but at this point I wondered why he should be married anymore. But Charlie would never give up on us. He would say, "I love you." That's that. I guess that's what motivated me to keep trying, too. We both loved each other, but the reality of the work makes it extremely difficult to maintain a relationship.

As I mentioned before, the Nassau County area around the apartment -- which bordered between Jamaica, Queens and Jamaica Estates -- decided to open some areas to lower income families and then the safety of the area started to change. People were selling drugs, or were on drugs themselves.

There were some good times around the apartment, too. The back of our apartment had a grassy field of yellow daisies that Jennifer liked to play with. She loved laying on them and, to this day, she still loves yellow sunflowers.

One day, I took Jennifer, who was almost three, to the park next to my apartment. I saw a girl reading a famous New York City newspaper, "The Village Voice," and I came up to her and asked, "Are you crazy or are you normal?" She said that she was crazy, and to this day we are still friends, even though she now lives in North Carolina. We still keep in touch.

Esther was her name. She and her husband, Al [who was very handsome and I always thought they were the perfect couple] lived on the opposite side of the park from me. Years later and after three children, they were divorced. Esther decided to legally changed her name to Grace. It took me years to get used to her new name.

I had finally made some friends. Esther and my next-door neighbor Donna and I had a lot of fun hanging out together. The two of them were pregnant at the same time, and I still picture them dancing in my apartment and bumping their stomachs together. I laughed so hard I had to literally run to the bathroom to pee. We took the kids out to McDonalds so they could go on the rides or just hang at each others places. We became great friends, which really helped me through the lonely times.

But again, things dramatically changed for me.

Esther and Abe decided to move to Virginia to start a new business. Abe was always into different kinds of business ventures, so after two years, they left. Soon after that, Donna and Todd also moved away, and I was alone again to figure out the next step.

I really wanted to move. The apartment was nice, but with my friends gone, I felt that I needed a change.

The final straw on deciding to move was one day, I was walking Jennifer in the stroller to the park and on the way back, there was a man following us. I was on the side of the apartment building near the garage door, and I turned around and this man was moving toward me and Jennifer. He was so close to us, that I could see his eyes were dilated. I started yelling, being loud so someone could see me from the window. I was so scared he was going to push me and the stroller down the garage stairs, but thankfully he turned and ran. We got back to the apartment and I said, "enough!" I have had enough.

When Charlie came home from touring, I told him: "Either we move or I am going back to Florida!"

We started our search for a house. Since I had my cousin Milton living in Levittown, a large community on Long Island, and my Aunt Lily who also lived in Old Westbury, Long Island, we looked toward that area.

We finally went farther east on Long Island in Suffolk County, about an hour from Manhattan. We came across a town called Centereach, which is near Port Jefferson, Stoneybrook University, East Hamptons, Montauk and heading West, Smithtown, and Oyster Bay.

We found our house pretty quickly in an established neighborhood on a quiet street off Nichols Road. My dad was a big help in getting us a second mortgage so we could close on the house. Years later, my dad gave us the second mortgage. That was nice of him.

It was a beautiful ranch house, with three bedrooms and three bathrooms, with a beautiful basement that had a round bar and all wood surrounding the bar. A large fenced yard with stairs going down from the open kitchen. The living-room was huge with a giant fire place.

In some ways, Charlie leaving for tour was good for me because I had to make a lot of choices on my own. On the other hand, feeling abandoned as years went by took an emotional toll on me again, even in the new house. It is so hard to feel loved when you husband's suitcase is next to your bed.

I would go on tour with Charlie off and on for a lot of years, just to keep this relationship strong, but I realized that I was the only one trying so hard. I was consumed and teased by the music, always so close but so far away from me. I needed some acceptance for what I could do, but I felt less important than his job. Music was still a part of me, just not how I wanted it to be. The feeling of inadequacy was still there, but I was working hard on overcoming these feelings.

I can't blame all of the problems on Charlie. I did make the commitment, but I also had to put my foot down on this one-sided relationship. I was not giving up and neither was Charlie. Things had to change, and finally they did.

Later on, I took Jennifer with me on a long flight to meet up with Charlie, who was coming in from Japan. The flight was long and, thankfully, I had a flight attendant helping me with Jennifer. Surprisingly, she did really well on the flight. This was my first time in Oahu. It was beautiful and our hotel was in Waikiki. I remember staring from our balcony at a pink hotel. We walked with Jennifer in a stroller to the waterfalls that were close. We had a wonder time, until Jennifer started getting sick and we ended up in the clinic, where she was diagnosed with bronchitis and was given antibiotics. I don't even remember the Hall and Oates show, but it was quite an adventure. We got a babysitter that was screened by the hotel so we could have a date night. We went to a Luau right on the beach and I had a long red sarong Hawaiian dress, and I must admit, it looked good. It was romantic and the food was delicious. The Hawaiian dancers were beautiful, so the whole night was a happy time for us.

We went back home after a week, and Charlie was going to be home for a while.

It is hard to explain that when Charlie is performing, it's like part of me is performing, too. I can feel how he is trying to express the sounds he makes to the audience, and I get into the Charlie mode. You need to feel something to connect. I could never explain why, but somewhere, living with this job for years you can lose that musical connection. I disconnected from Charlie musically and was feeling more alone and isolated because it just seemed like it was not important to Charlie, but it sure was important to me. When he put out the effort, I could feel the connection again, but when he is just playing the notes, I could feel that too.

When I wrote a song and Charlie would arrange and play it, I would say to myself, "that felt amazing!"

I would get insulted if people asked me, "So, you were a groupie when you met Charlie?" This statement was so far from who I am and why we were together in the first place. I would bite my lip and not say anything back.

The good thing is that I am not dependent on Charlie or anyone now, Financially, I would be okay. When he puts out the effort, I feel important again, and that's something you cannot put into words. Today, Charlie has been trying to do that. You must have some things in common and a musical connection to keep this kind of relation going strong. It is so important. In my opinion, if you don't start feeling you have something in common, you are in trouble. I think that was one of the things that kept us together all these years.

The following is more of my Journal, so you may read a little more detailed information that I already wrote about.

Journal, December, 1982

Long Island, Music & April

As we were searching for a house, I found out I was pregnant again. We were both happy and wanted a sibling for Jennifer and it was perfect timing, we thought. So, we decided to search on Long Island far enough that we could afford a house and we came across a place in Centereach, New York in the eastern part of Long Island. This particular neighborhood was an old established area where families had been there for a long time and then the children took over the houses their parents lived in. This particular street we found was on Drake Road, and most of the houses reminded me of the house I grew up in.

The street was quiet with a lot of big trees, and the house we spotted was a brown ranch style design. As you come up the walkway, there were three flights of stairs. As soon as you walk into the front door there is a huge living room with a fireplace and dining room combined. To the left from the hall or the dining room was a a large kitchen with a gas stove and a place for a kitchen table. I was afraid of the stove since I only used electric, but I guess I will have to get used to it. There were sliding glass doors leading downstairs to a quarter-acre back yard which had lots of trees for Charlie to sneeze at, since he is allergic to a lot of different types of trees. Walking back up the stairs past the kitchen on your right was a door leading down to a huge and completed basement with beautiful wood through-out and a large bar matching the all oak wood walls.

Going back into the house through the kitchen to a hallway past the door to the basement were three bedroom and two bathrooms.

We really liked the house, but how can we afford to pay for it? We definitely loved the house, so we agreed and were able to get a mortgage, and my dad was kind enough to help us with the second mortgage with arrangements to pay him back. I had some savings, so the decision was made. On December 12, 1982, we moved to our first house and major investment.

The memories on Drake Road were many, from the birth of our second daughter to seeing our first snow coming down, and taking the snow and making snow cones ... putting chocolate syrup on the snow which was fresh and soft, and then coming in for hot chocolate. We became friends with our neighbors, Kitty and Ron, with their two children, and down the street were two other families, Sally and her family. Then around the block was a family whose cousin was the famous photographer, Edward Steichen.

Sometimes the kids would go down to the sump and use cardboard or anything they could find that would help them slide down the hill in the snow.

During the holidays, I would drive the kids to the end of the street to wait for the fire truck to come around with Santa Claus on top of the truck. He would throw candy canes to all the kids in the neighborhood.

I really loved Oxhead Elementary, where Jennifer went. We have never forgotten Mrs. Berman, who was an outstanding teacher. She made going to school a lot of fun for the kids, like making a witch's brew on Halloween, and then all the children would march around the school in their costumes. The inside cafeteria became an art project for all of the families to paint and draw on the walls to make it colorful. I am pretty sure the large paintings are still there. Past the school was this high hill that felt like a roller coaster when you drove up it. People said the hill was haunted.

We would go out to eastern Long Island to an amazing farm that made homemade pies, called Briar Farms. The pies were huge and the bakery smelled so good that you didn't know which pie to choose.

Our other family outing was to a restaurant called The Elbow Room, where people from all over the world would come and have their famous marinated steak that had a secret sauce that made the outside a charcoal black topping, but moist pink center on the inside. Later on, we found one of the secret ingredients was a spice called Beau Monde.

We would often visit a beautiful quaint town 20 minutes from us, Port Jefferson, which was on the North Shore and a short walk to Long Island Sound, where the Ferries would go back and forth from Bridgeport, Connecticut. You can also take the ferry at the end of Long Island from Montauk to Mystic Seaport, Connecticut, which is a really pretty area of shops, private boats and restaurants. From there, you could drive about four hours to Boston all the way to Maine.

The ferry in Port Jefferson was across the street on the corner that was called the "Steam Room." Delicious fresh fish of all kinds was served. You would order at the counter and then sit outside in the summer watching the ferry or just people-watch, or you could sit inside by the fire in the winter.

Charlie and I saw and ad in the paper for a piano that someone wanted to sell in Port Jefferson for $500. We ended up getting the piano, and it had been with us ever since.

Another memorable special place in Port Jefferson was a private recording studio for bands like Foghat, or Tom Petty, and it was called at first the Boogie Motel, which was the name from one of Foghat's albums. Boogie Motel became a commercial studio in 1980 with a small change to The Boogie Hotel. This was a beautiful Victorian mansion built in 1751, and later a theater was added for performances. The sound quality of the recordings was excellent. For example, it had a live echo chamber that was installed and quite a few selections of tube and recording microphones. Upstairs were five bedrooms and a place to create music. The main floor had a large living room, café and a full kitchen. The outside had a beautiful wrap-around porch which was used quite a lot in those days. I saw Tom Petty recording there, which was very impressive.

My second memory was being in the studio while the great R&B singer, songwriter Don Covay [whose songs were recorded by Aretha Franklin, Chubby Checker, Gladys Knight and the Pips and the Rolling Stones] was doing a remake of his famous song, "Chain of Fools." Someone asked me to sing the high background part and they liked it, but I was told that I had to wait for the manager to hear and approve the vocal but he had already left. Darn it, I was so close to recording a well-known song. Oh Well, that was my almost one minute of fame. It was still a great experience that I will always remember. Sadly, on February 5, 2015, Don Covay passed away.

Years later, Charlie was playing a gig on Long Island and there were some singers and they were going to sing "Chain of Fools." I got up and sang with them and, boy, was that a rush for me hearing my sound blending with the band. It was a joy to be part of a band for a short time. I can understand the thrill to have a unified sound that works. You can't explain the feeling.

The second day in our house, there was a bad snow storm. Charlie couldn't work the coal stove that was in the fireplace and our house got really smokey. He finally figured out how to open the fire vent which was in the chimney. We are from Florida, so what did we know about fire places?

After that, the tub drain was clogged so... welcome to being a new home owner.

I wasn't feeling excited or happy, just kind of numb from moving and being pregnant. But still, it was nice to have our own place for once that was ours.

This pregnancy was a little harder than the first one, and it seems I developed some asthma and a constant stuffed up nose...Yuk! I am hoping this baby will be okay with some of the medicine the doctor gave me for the congestion.

On December 20th 1982, I felt the baby flutter in my stomach, I was having a little anxiety again, but I am coping better. I was still worried about hurting the baby with the cold medicine. Finally, the house is slowly getting cleaner, but I have to adjust to Charlie going on tour again for four months. Yes, I said four months.

January 25, 1983

Charlie is downstairs writing a Hall and Oates chart out but I surprisingly felt much better, even though Charlie was leaving soon. I do feel a little scared being alone that long a time, and sometimes depressed, but I must find some more activities by going to the Mother's Center and going to a Prenatal class for exercising once a week. I needed to do something else. My mind kept thinking, music, music, music.

The baby is moving more and I feel some small contractions, which must be Braxton Hicks. So, I knew this was normal.

I have two names for the baby, "Ian" if it is a boy, and "April" if it is a girl. Charlie liked both. I was still getting used to the house and I really liked it, but it gets so quiet.

Jennifer is so cute at three-years-old. She's really into monsters, and her favorite word is "sexy." When she is laying with me, she will start snapping her fingers. She developed that skill when she was eight-months-old. I have her in nursery school at Miss Barbara's. It is close to the house where she went three times a week. She is very sensitive, and all kinds of things scare her at this age.

March, 1983

I was six months pregnant at the time when I took another one of my trips to see Charlie with Jennifer.

Charlie was in Baltimore, so I drove my car to Islip airport and flew to Baltimore to be with him for a few days.

After the show, we went to the hotel and, lying in bed, I heard on the news that a blizzard was heading for Baltimore. I told Charlie around 2 a.m. that I had better get out of here since I was not going on to the next city, which would have cost us more in airfare if I would have stayed. I was tired and wanted to get home.

The Baltimore airport was closed, so Jennifer and I got on the train taking us back to Penn Station for the transfer to another train heading for Islip Airport. Of course, wouldn't you know it, the blizzard heading for Baltimore turned toward New York City and, by the time I got, there, bam! The storm hit Manhattan.

You can picture a pregnant woman with a three-year-old getting on a train full of commuters, also trying to get home in the middle of a snow storm. I had to figure out how to get back to my car.

I was so lucky to have talked to someone on the train who could drive me from the Islip train stop to the airport parking lot, which was now closed due to the storm.

There was my car, buried in snow, and me with Jennifer trying to help unbury the car. I was exhausted, crabby, and this was not fun for either one of us, as you can imagine.

Charlie was calling me, but I had no time to talk to him. I had to be careful driving back with the hard snow, wind and the slippery streets. I was so glad to be home, and Charlie called again and I said, "We've got to talk."

When Charlie came home, I told him, "you can stay here, but I am going back to Florida." I was done with snow, digging out of snow, slippery roads, and freezing temperatures. Not only the weather, but the property taxes were being raised. We found out the town next to ours were increasing to almost $6,000. It was time to move.

Charlie realized that he could still do his job, even though we moved. Truthfully, we realized we could have stayed in Florida from the beginning. However, management wanted him in New York for some reason. I guess to save on air-fare of flying him back and forth.

When Charlie went on tour, he continued writing letters or calling about what he was doing. It is fun to see new places, but the down time can cause boredom and loneliness for both of us sometimes. He set up a keyboard in the hotel room so he can continue doing his own songs, read, or go out with the guys to eat.

When Jennifer is in school, I would also go turn on the keyboard I had downstairs in the basement, or start writing down stories that were geared toward children.

I still have problems with the asthmas returning for this pregnancy, but the doctor thinks it is just temporary because of the baby growing. I am a lot bigger with this baby than I was with Jennifer. I am eight months pregnant now, and I gained 17 pounds, which is good, the doctor said. I am feeling good, considering Charlie is gone and I have spurts of energy, then bouts of being tired. Again, like my first pregnancy, my hair got thick and my nails, which are usually brittle, were nice and strong.

Sleeping became more difficult waking up with a bloody nose and the baby kicking more and more.

One night, when Charlie was home, I was lying in bed and I was staring at my stomach and, oh my, we could see the outline of the baby's foot moving across my stomach. That was really neat to see.

Jennifer and I went on tour with Charlie, so we drove to Allentown, Pennsylvania, Hershey and Philadelphia. It was our seven-year wedding anniversary and 11 years total we have been together. Jennifer had bronchitis but she's okay now.

New York City was the next stop where Hall and Oates played Madison Square Garden and, oh my! The baby was kicking up a storm heading to Manhattan, and there was there was the baby's foot gliding across my stomach as I am watching Charlie play his famous solo part in the song, "No Can Do." This was a total surprise when he got three standing ovations, and I had hoped there would be some great review of his playing, but for some reason, the management did not acknowledge Charlie's performance. I was so disappointed that not one person said anything, as far as I knew.

June 7, 1983

Charlie started rehearsals yesterday and was not sure whether to go or not, since I was so close to the due date, but at this stage financially we couldn't rock the boat or get fired, so he had to go. I understood. I tried to keep busy by getting a new water bed, putting Jennifer into gymnastics and spending a lot of time at the library. Our library had wonderful programs for Jennifer, like sign language, art, music. I had a lot of energy at this point, so doing chores was easy and kept me busy, even going on the piano while Jennifer was sleeping.

I started having Braxton Hicks about seven minutes apart, but no labor yet. The worst part is the due date had come and gone. Charlie had to leave in three days for the tour, so I don't think he is going to make it to the birth. The baby was way overdue. We were both worried that he would have to leave, and he did. I had a lot of support, so that was good. But don't get me wrong, it was hard without him.

My dad came in from his Israel trip, thinking I had the baby, but this little one wanted to stay with me as long as possible. That was good that he was here just in case, or I would have been home with Jennifer alone, and she was sick with a stuffy nose...poor thing.

Things we got for the house was working out nicely. We got the water bed and then a new VCR and a typewriter. I could start typing out stories and lyrics again, which I liked to do. I was also planning on doing lyrics and poems, but the tour put a little damper on my plans. I am a survivor, and Charlie was not very happy that he had to leave.

Going into Labor with April was much easier and more exciting, and boy, did I want the baby to come and hopefully, very soon.

The day I went into Labor, my dad stayed with me and we invited my Aunt Celia and Aunt Lily, my dad's sisters, to come and visit. I remember us waiting for them, but I had to go to the bathroom and...uh, oh, my water broke.

Since I was experience with having Jennifer, I knew it would be a while before I needed to go to the hospital, so I came out and met my aunts at the front door with my dad and said, "hello everyone, I'm in labor!" Well, you should have seen their faces. It would have been a great YouTube video.

I told them not to worry, so we all talked for a while, but you could see they were ready to jump from the table at any time. They were more nervous than me. Finally, my dad talked me into going to the hospital. My contractions were not that bad, but we ended up going.

We got to Smithtown General Hospital and checked in. The waiting began.

The doctor came in and said I have plenty of time and I was about 4 centimeters so he said he was going to see his patients and not to worry. Charlie would be on the phone with me, and I would try to talk to him in-between contractions. Then Charlie did the show, so by that time I couldn't talk to him anymore.

Since Charlie was not there, my neighbor, Lauren, who had four children, came with me for support. Of course, my dad was there, too. Jennifer was being watched at home with a neighbor. I don't remember much after that, but by early evening, I was hurting [since I did not take any pain medicine or epidural].

When the doctor broke my water, April came into this world an hour later -- on June 12, 1983 at 7:45 p.m. at eight pounds. But I had a problem after the birth. She came out screaming and turning bright red. I saw the nurse put her in the bassinet, and she was grabbing the sides and wouldn't let go. The nurse looked at me and started smiling, saying she just didn't want to come out. Luckily, instead of a 34-hour intense labor I had with Jennifer; April came out in eight hours.

I just wouldn't stop bleeding. The doctor looked at me and asked if I felt like I was going to pass out. I said no, so they gave me a medication of Pitocin, which is usually given before the birth to help my uterus to contract more because I was bleeding a lot. The Pitocin finally worked, but it hurt a lot. Dad was standing outside of the door, I was told, and he was really worried. The bleeding finally stopped.

April's crying finally calmed down, especially when I put her on my stomach.

Meanwhile, Charlie was on stage. I guess the road manager got a message to him, and they got him on the next flight out right after the show. He got in the very next morning. We were so happy that he made it pretty fast. I got up from my bed and Charlie kissed us both, then got in my bed holding April... and would you believe he fell asleep holding her? What a sight that was, as I was standing over them. Wait a minute, who just gave birth? I wish I would have had my camera to take a picture of the two of them.

Jennifer came in later in the day and she seemed happy to see her little sister, but she was very happy to see me, too. A little stressful and confusing for an almost four-year-old.

Jennifer was so happy to have a sister. She was always watching me when I took care of April. She was very excited and so full of all kinds of emotions and a strong love for me but she didn't seem jealous.

April was a very independent little baby and did not like it when I tried to cuddle her or hug her -- unless she was sick -- but sometimes, when you least expect it, as she got older, she would crawl up on my lap and just want me to hold her, which made me happy. I really loved her, especially when she came to me, which was not often. She watched Jennifer, and followed her a lot, and Jennifer loved being the big sister.

Our family was complete and we decided not to have an more children because of my health issues, finances, and Charlie going away a lot. I still wondered how it would have been if I had a boy, but my two beautiful girls made me happy.

When April was about seven months old, when went to a family reunion in the northern part of the state called, Renovo, Pennsylvania, near Lock Haven in the mountains [where Charlie lived when he was very young]. Later, some of his family moved to Florida. It was wonderful to see everyone. I really liked his family. They were so different than mine. Very laid back and sweet people.

I don't think April was feeling good, and I started wondering if there was a problem with her stomach.

Months later, we took a trip to Disney World. From January to March, Charlie was on a long tour again.

Mary 26,1984

I was turning 35 tomorrow. Saying I am that old feels strange to me. I feel young and old at the same time. I started feeling distant with Charlie and feeling so far away from doing music, songs, dance, fun, love and happiness. Sounds like a song in the making.

I still hope things will get better and I can start doing some things for myself. I did make one promise to myself that, after what happened to Jennifer, I would not go too far from them.

I brought two wonderful children into this world and, with Charlie gone again, I made them my first priority.

Charlie had a better chance of working than I did at this point. We did not have the money for childcare or daycare, so I always took advantage at nighttime to try and sing downstairs when I could. I even put in a local ad for a piano player. I forgot her name, but we did some songs together. Unfortunately, she was going to school and teaching, so it ended after a few months.

April is two-years-old and started to have stomach issues again. I was beginning to really worry about her. We took her to the doctor and did a complete exam with full blood test, including hypothyroid, x-rays and our family history. The final diagnosis was irritable bowel syndrome, which does run in my family. Soon after, she developed an ear infection, so she was put on antibiotic. We decided to wait and see if she would grow out of her stomach issues.

It was around this time that we had to put our dog, Lady, to sleep. She could barely walk or see, and we knew she had cancer. I took her on a final walk, and then we brought her to the vet. It was hard to say goodbye to her. She was with us from almost the beginning of my relationship with Charlie in my 20s. She always kept me company when Charlie was gone, being there when I had the girls. We had quite a history together. She was with me and Charlie for 14 years. I loved her, and she will be missed.

Oh, Lady

The look in your eyes
I will remember her well
You spoke through those eyes
I sometimes understand what you mean
You've been a friend
Who kept loneliness out
I will always remember
You sweet soul
Running around the house
You will be missed
Goodbye Lady, my friend

Our first dog, Lady.

I have never been without a dog, so months later, I took Jennifer to the North Shore Animal League. I saw this sweet collie mix staring at me, and I took her out of the cage while looking at other animals. We knew this was the one; we named her Sara. She was quite a sweet girl, but she was so frightened of storms that she would shiver in fright. She was really good with the girls.

Later on, I went to a breeder and I got a West Highland Terrier and we named her Kasey. Years later, we thought that Kasey was not a very bright dog and wouldn't follow simple command, but I took her for a checkup and we found out she was deaf. I felt so guilty not knowing, but it didn't seem too bother her. She was a very quiet, loving dog to everyone. Years later, we bred her and the whole family, including Sara, was there in our kitchen watching Kasey give birth to seven snowball puppies. This was such a wonderful event, and the girls were excited to see the puppies being born. The puppies stayed with us for almost two months. It was so much fun seeing all of them running down the backyard stairs and playing in the yard.

It was time to sell the puppies and we almost kept one, but the girls would not agree to be responsible for taking care of another pet. It was sad to see the puppies go.

The beginning of the 90s came, so I started working on my vocals again, practicing in the basement every chance I got... but it was so hard keeping the practice up that, eventually, I couldn't do it anymore. But it felt great to get back into singing again.

January 6, 1985

April is 18 months, and Jennifer is almost five and currently into gymnastics, which she seemed to like. Sadly, I took the girls to the last part of the "Big Bam Boom," tour in Denver. This was also the time that April was still having stomach issues.

January 22, 1985

I finally had enough of April's stomach problem, and nothing seemed to help, so the doctor decided to do a biopsy to see if she possibly had celiac disease. The following letter is what I wrote to the doctor on how horrible this situation was handled. I hope no one had to go through what we had to deal with in trying to help April with her stomach pain at such a young age. I was feeling helpless and hated seeing her in pain. The following is a letter I wrote to give you an idea of what we went through:

Dear Dr. Partin:

I want to thank you for sending us a letter concerning my daughter, April. It showed me the lack of communication there had been throughout her illness. I did take April to North Shore Hospital, and she was seen by another doctor and a resident. I was very happy with the complete examination they did on her, which was a complete blood work and family history. The final diagnosis was irritable bowel syndrome, which does run in my family. April is to be checked again in two months for weight changes. Two days after we saw the doctor, April developed an ear infection and was put on antibiotic. Her pain after two days subsided. A week after she finished her antibiotic, everything started again-- plus a stuffy nose -- and also some of her teeth were coming in.

According to your letter, we have been complaining about your means to finding out what April's problem could be. We never complained-- we merely needed to know how to help her, and if this was the best way to find out what the issues are. We are very concerned and just want the best for her. I can't understand why a complete work-up and family history was not done first and to look at other possible causes for her pain. The next step was a biopsy.

According to the doctor, no special controlled diet was necessary before this biopsy was done, yet you said she need to be hospitalized to control her diet. He also said a tube would be put down April's throat and bile would be collected with no sedation. We were told differently when we spoke to the nurse that was at the hospital the night we admitted her. I feel the procedure was not explained to us properly, and of if any risks were involved. We didn't realize how invasive the procedure was going to be, and the doctor sounded like it was an easy procedure and not too worry. When the nurse explained to us that they will be cutting a part of her, I basically freaked out and took her out of the hospital without their consent. I am so glad I did.

In you last paragraph, you stated that, "if I was managing this patient, I would be content to follow her weight, height, and hemogram, as well as proceed with an examination of the stools on a monthly basis for the next two or three months. If growth is normal and the symptomatic complaints subside, not further work-up is indicated."

Why wasn't this told to us? We also weren't sure that my daughter's problem could last much longer, since she showed such continued pain for quite a long time. All we were concerned about is this continuous problem of distention and the best way to help her through this.

I hope by writing this letter, you understand that we, as parents, have the right to know all possible ways and alternatives for the best treatment possible. I never thought asking questions was considered doubting someone's professionalism.

The reason for this letter was never being told what the biopsy procedure entailed. When we heard the details, we walked out of the hospital. It was the best decision we made.

We continued monitoring April, and by putting her on a stricter diet, she finally she started to get better. I am sure she had a sensitive stomach, like me, and the next step was to figure out what was triggering the pain, which we did.

This was definitely an eye-opening experience to always search out other options if it entails an invasive procedure that could be dangerous. Basically, go with your instincts, get another opinion, and ask other parents their ideas. If you feel something is wrong, it probably is, unless proven otherwise.

April 15, 1983

The girls and I went on tour with Charlie to Detroit and Chicago, since it was around our nine-year wedding anniversary, and we had a really nice time at the Saint Regis in Chicago.

I met JJ. Jackson, who was an American soul and R&B singer, songwriter and arranger. He is better known for the song, "But It's Alright."

I also met Martha Quinn, who was well know as one of the original video jockeys on MTV. She was so sweet, and came by our hotel room to see April and Jennifer, but they were sleeping.

I have been feeling unhappy lately. I love the kids, but as I get older, I feel my relationship with Charlie is so one-sided sometimes. It seems like I give and give. I was exhausted and tired, trying to hold the marriage together with the traveling, and making sure the girls are okay and not doing anything creatively, it gets me frustrated a lot. I always thought marriage was a mutual bond of give-and-take. I started feeling badly that my family didn't get to know the real me or they just didn't want to. A little sad at times, but I am trying to accept that, and sticking with my decision to move on and try my best.

Charlie was still a sweet guy, and he was content with the relationship, but felt he had no choice in the situation he was in financially.

Jennifer is now five-and-a-half-years-old and so grown and beautiful. She's quite a sweet daughter. I am glad she is with me.

April is 22-months-old and getting bigger and she does such cute things at this age. She is such a joy and full of curiosities at this time, but what a temper she has when she gets angry. But she is trying to understand the world around her and to make sure she is heard.

May 6, 1986

I can't believe almost a year has passed since I started writing. I am now 36, Jennifer is six-and-a-half and April is almost three.

This was not an easy time for the family. Especially with the passing of my father, April 20, 1986. At 75. We just saw him three weeks earlier for his 75th birthday party at my sister's house in Miami. I still feel numb and one part of me wouldn't accept his death. It makes you think of the past and a sense of lost by saying, "I don't have a father anymore." Yet, sadly, we did not have a great relationship.

The only good thing that happen at this time was my dad hearing a song I wrote called, "Dreams," which Charlie recorded. That was a nice feeling to hear my song being played. It was a small step for me, but an important one.

After the passing of my dad, my sister went in for gall bladder surgery and everything went well for her.

Charlie and I started having strong thoughts of moving back to Florida -- in particular, Orlando, because there seems to be more local jobs and promises of working at the convention center, hotels or local clubs in the area. Where else could we go for more job opportunities and still be in Florida? It was tough to decide to make the move, but one warning for us to seriously consider leaving were the property taxes in our area. Those were increasing and getting really expensive.

Our 10th wedding anniversary was a month ago. Charlie was back from touring, so we decided to get away for some fun and decided to have someone watch the girls so we could go to the Pocono Mountains to a place called Cove Haven, which is a resort open year-round for adults.

It was still cold and snowing when we got up there and checked into our room.

The room was really nice on three levels. You walk in to the first level -- the living-room -- which had a small pool right there. Then you looked up to the second level, there was a champagne shaped jacuzzi bath made of clear plexiglass with a surrounding balcony so you can look down at the first level. On the opposite side of the bathtub was a huge bed, and we laughed when we looked up and saw a mirror above the bed. From the living room you go down one flight and there is a nice size sauna room.

The center of the resort was a huge restaurant and bar, where most couple go for dinner and shows. I am not much of a drinker, but the bartender made me drink called Sombrero, which was basically a White Russian with ice cream it. Delicious!

Charlie and I decided to try a snow mobile for the first time. He drove the mobile and I was on the back. He sure was a dare devil, but it was a lot of fun.

April graduated nursery school at Commack Coop and we signed her up with swimming classes at the YMCA. She put her head under water with no problem, and I was so proud of her. I liked the way they taught swimming. They started with using at least three baby floaters on each arm and, as the child becomes more comfortable and swims, they slowly take off one floater at a time. After a week or so, both April and Jennifer learned to swim very quickly with no drama.

One day I was watching the girls swim at the pool and I heard my name being called. That surprised me, since I did not know anyone. So I thought I was just hearing things. But I looked up and was so surprised to see one of my childhood friends looking at me. It was Carolyn, who was the one who had the house in Coral Gables near me, whose father took us to the race-track. I was so happy to see her. What a small world it was.

One day Jennifer handed me this really sweet mommy letter. My heart just melted when I read it.

At this time, touring had ended and, luckily, they put Charlie on retainer -- but we were not sure if and when touring would start again. You never know in this business, and you feel a little scared of what is going to happen next.

Charlie was really helpful to me during Dad's passing and the end of tour-ing. We have been getting along much better. He took over most of the child-care and housework from September to May so I could graduate college. At first, he wanted to go hang out with his friend, Buddy, who came into town so they could play music, but I finally put my foot down and said this is not going to happen. I have to finish school so I can do some teaching and make some money while he was not working.

I went back to college at Old Westbury University, which had another college program called, Empire State College. The great thing about this program is that they took prior experiences like music, composing, writing stories, dance, prior substitute teaching which gave me credit for what they called, "life experiences." After adding up my credentials, I only needed a year plus student teaching to get my bachelor of science degree. That is the degree level they put me under. Hooray! I finally started to work on my own career while Charlie was home.

I was accepted to Chestnut Hill Elementary for my student teaching, which was a requirement for graduating. I was under a wonderful teacher, Roberta Opas. I really enjoyed the students. It was a bittersweet last day when I finished and she gave me a beautiful note and a gift. To this day, I still remember her kindness.

I did start substitute teaching at different schools in the area, but I was not happy teaching for some reason. I didn't feel challenged and I got bored very quickly. I loved the children, but I wanted to create. Teaching was taking me away from the typewriter and composing, and I felt like Charlie and I were pulling farther apart unless I kept up with him and when touring started again.

I think anxiety was slowly creeping up on me and I was trying to be both a mom, wife of a musician and keeping my own self-worth intact. The worst situation that happened to me is when I was going to meet Charlie in New Orleans and my stomach was killing me. The plane made a stop-over and I couldn't go back onto the plane. I went back home while Charlie was waiting for me at the airport. I called to let him know that I went back home and went to the doctor, and he said I had an infection. I was put on a strict diet of no milk, sugar, honey or yeast. I was feeling really sick and I started thinking about my own mortality and what to tell my daughters.

A Note to my Daughters

Remember, you both will continue where Charlie and I left off, and you carry us within you because we are a part of each other. You are not alone. Every single person goes through some hard times on your journey. Our love is in both of you and your children to come. Like my father said to me, "you are both beautiful Jewels that we created." I love both of you so much. Death is sad but I would rather you both celebrate our life with music and funny stories that you can tell your children. I am so glad that you have each other for the rest of your lives, even if you live in different places. I am so grateful and I appreciate the family I do have. I have written this journal to both of you to keep my spirit alive as you read my thoughts on these pages. Music and family: who could ask for anything more?

Charlie stopped working for Hall and Oates. They decided not to tour, so Charlie was on his own to find gigs on Long Island, where he got to meet some wonderful musicians. Eventually, Charlie got a job in the city working for Ascap, which is a professional organization of songwriters, composers and music publishers -- owned and run by members -- to make sure artists were paid royalties for their work. This was a business that license songs and scores to the businesses that play them publicly, then send the money to the members as royalties. This is what Charlie did for the next few years, traveling by train five days a week, near Lincoln Center.

Then one day Hall and Oates asked Charlie to come back.

I am sorry if I sound like this type of lifestyle is all bad, but it's not. There were some memorable times as well that I can share with you.

Adjusting to the tour schedule when I go on the road is very important, because if you are late, everyone else is late, so it is a group effort -- and I have to also work within certain time frames. Everyone gets an itinerary of each day's schedule, from when you leave, sound-check, dinner time, etc. Nothing changes from the itinerary unless the road manager gives you a heads up that there is a change. After the show, either we go back to the hotel or get on the bus to the next city. The demands of the job should not take away from my commitment to Charlie, no matter what. So, I adjusted accordingly.

There is a lot of great things about being on tour, especially if you have some down time to see some of the sights, and an extra bonus if we stay in one place for two or three days.

I enjoy sound check because if there is a piano back stage in one of the rooms, I can play while they are rehearsing. I used to watch them rehearse, but most of the time, the audio tech is testing the sound system for each artist and making sure the lighting cues are set. Then some songs are played -- usually without Daryl, but John always comes to rehearse. This usually goes on for about an hour, then the waiting starts.

Before April was born, I would sometimes take Jennifer on the road with me when she was around two and even traveled on the tour bus for short trips. I remember when Mickey Curry [who was a drummer with Cher, Tina Turner, Alice cooper, David Bowie, Elvis Costello and Bryan Adams] would sit in the front seat of the bus and would hold Jennifer while she slept. He was so sweet to her. They guys didn't seem to mind that we were there. I guess it sometimes nice to have a new face cheer everyone up with these tedious drives.

They were all a band family to Charlie and me. Of course, a lot of the musicians were not permanent members for some reason or another. We would get used to everyone, and then they would be gone after one or two years.

The organization was always making changes, but we did not know why some musicians were let go. We were never told, but maybe it was better that way. You never know, it could have been Charlie at one point. Sometimes the main artists just want a change and reaching for different sounds, so you can't take it personally. But at the same time, it does hurt when you are financially scraping by. That is the nature of the business.

I was pretty much by myself whenever I would go with Charlie unless the kids came, which was very rare. I would sometimes meet him at different venues. This had been going on for over 43 years now.

I had adapted to different situations and learned a lot about what goes on before and even after the shows. This was definitely a unique position I was in, getting to know the musicians, or the crew that helps make the music so vibrant. Taking care of the lighting, setting up the stage, loading and unloading the trucks of equipment, working on the side of the stage, handling different instruments for the performers before, during and after the show, always on the alert if something happens during the show such as monitor problems or musicians not hearing themselves while performing. There is the theatre staff helping the performers with wardrobe, pressing stage clothes or alterations that need to be done, and the caterers making and feeding a lot of people to make sure the food choices have a lot of healthy options to choose from. The road manager, who makes sure everyone knows what is going on and checking to make sure the artists and performers are accounted for, guiding the musicians on and off the stage, plus helping with ticketing and getting in and out of the venue as smooth as possible before and after the show.

These are talented people behind the scenes that people do not get to see. After the show, everything has to be torn down, loaded into trucks for traveling the same night to the next show and starting the whole process over and over, night after night, until the end of the tour. Does it get boring sometimes? Yes, it does, but the music makes it all worthwhile.

The managers would come in once in a while to see if everything is running smoothly.

One time they had hired me to sell merchandise in the lobby but Charlie got me fired. No kidding, he really did.

He would come out after the show to where I was, and that did not work well with the person running the merchandise. Oh, well, it was a good experience, and I could say I worked for Hall and Oates. Ha!

If you think about it, this is all because two artists got together and wrote and played songs, and the many years it took too be finally heard. Every organization on the road has different methods on putting on a show, but pretty much do the same thing to get the whole show to work.

There is a lot of waiting around before a show, and if you wonder what is going on with the band, truthfully not much. The band usually pass the time practicing on their instruments, talking to family on their iPhones or to each other about music or working on their lap tops. You can hear a lot of great stories about their adventures with other fellow musicians they had worked with.

The main performers usually come in later to connect with the band members before a show, or they will meet and greet family, friends and fans after the show. There is a lot of energy, and everyone seems to enjoy the adrenaline of the crowd while waiting to either go on the bus to the next city or back to the hotel if they are staying over.

I was fortunate enough to be allowed, at times, to travel with the guys, whether in limos, vans or tour buses. I really enjoyed listening to all the stories over the years, but I will always respect everyone's privacy and keep my dis-

Sheila with Jennifer

tance when a private conversation is going on. While on the bus, I will be with everyone for a while but then, not to disturb their routine, I would head to the back with my iPad, play music or watch television. I could never sleep on the bus. I enjoyed conversations with everyone in the band, and they would talk to me sometime about music and treated me as a friend who also contributed a little to music.

Charlie liked for me to come sometimes because he knew I would adjust to their schedules, such as being down at the lobby of the hotel at a certain time, or leaving back to the hotel when everyone was ready to go.

I must admit that I started getting bored again on the road, hearing the music being played over and over. Watching them play was sometimes like a job, only with no feeling behind it. I could tell the difference when someone is playing with emotion or just playing the song while thinking of something else. Once in a while, you can hear the emotional side come out on stage and I loved that. To give you an example, try learning a song. At first you really like it, and then you play it 500 times … and you can't change anything. It has to be played exactly as written, which can become tedious.

Charlie is really good at bringing some different feels to the song when he solos. Throwing in some jazz always helps and gets the audience on its feet.

The best thing is the feedback from the audience, which really helps a lot to bring new energy on stage.

Thanks to the fans for their enthusiasm. it is greatly appreciated.

MEETING DICK CLARK AND CELEBRITIES

The 70s and 80s were an exciting time for Hall and Oates. Their popularity grew, and offers started coming in for television appearances. They were asked to perform for Dick Clark on the show, "American Bandstand." The show was a popular way to showcase many famous bands. If you get on the show, you know you've made to the big-time.

I was allowed to go with Jennifer, who was two-years-old at the time. We were with Charlie backstage while everyone was having makeup done for the cameras, and in walks Dick Clark. He looked at me and saw Jennifer, and said he wanted to interview Jennifer while we were sitting on the bleachers during the show, especially when Hall and Oates perform. The bleachers are where the audience sits while the bands perform. I said yes, but then I thought about it later and worried that Jennifer may not understand what he was saying. She was just learning to talk. I was a little worried about that.

The show started, and Hall and Oates were introduced and played one song. Meanwhile, Dick Clark was sitting behind Jennifer and me, surrounded by the audience on the bleachers. He asked Jennifer who did she like best: Daryl, John or anybody else? Well, Jennifer looked at me and said "Daryl," but then she said, "anybody else." Everybody laughed and then Jennifer said, "Daddy" after I whispered it into her ears. Dick Clark said, "she will know daddy's name one day." I knew she did not understand his question and, of course, she knew her daddy. That was a memorable experience and luckily, I still have the tape of that particular show.

Years later, when I was at the Rock and Roll Hall of Fame in Ohio, they had old Dick Clark "American Bandstand" shows. One taping was Hall and Oates, but they did not show the interview of Jennifer. That was such a cute moment.

During my time on the road, I did get to meet some well-known performers. Some of them I liked and some I didn't. When some famous entertainers would come backstage where we were sitting, Charlie would introduce me. Some of them were not very cordial; truthfully, I thought many were snobby. There were some people that I did like, though. I was never impressed by who you were, but if you were nice, even though I wasn't a celebrity. For example, I met Gilda Radner. She was married for a short time to G.E. Smith, the Hall and Oates guitar player at that time [who later became part of the Saturday Night Live band and other touring bands].

One day, I was sitting back stage and Gilda came by me and sweetly tapped me on the head and said, "poor Sheila." Later on, I understood what she meant. I knew her relationship with G.E. would not last and, sure enough, a few years later they got divorced. I really liked her and I was so happy when she met Gene Wilder, a great comedic actor. I thought they made a wonderful couple. I felt really bad when she passed away from cancer years later.

Do you recall reading earlier in the book that I went to school with Gilda's back-up singers for her Broadway show that Charlie and I got to see? It truly is a small world that I would meet Gilda under different circumstances.

On July 4, 1985, what a memorable experience I had. Charlie and I flew in a helicopter to Liberty State Park, New Jersey from Manhattan as we hovered over the Skyscrapers toward the island for a benefit concert to restore the Statue of Liberty. Quite a thrill flying over the city. We all got off and I noticed David Lee Roth was in another helicopter next to ours. At first, we were taken to a trailer where I could see outside as people walked by. There was Jack Nicholson walking past the trailer. For some reason, he gave me the creeps.

Later on, we were taken to a huge tent and, as I walked in, there were the

Rolling Stones. I remember looking at Mick Jagger, thinking how strange his face was, and I definitely wouldn't have dated him if I wasn't married. I am sure he probably was a nice guy, but not my type.

Eventually, Hall and Oates were called to go on, so I followed to the side of the stage where I was taken by surprise at the thousands of people watching and waiting for the show to begin. It was quite a sight from my view point. I would have had a panic attack if I was performing, so I am sure everyone was nervous and excited at the same time. During the show, I got to see Tina Turner and the Rolling Stones perform, and then at the end of the shows the fireworks lit up the sky, the jets flew over, and the beautiful red, white and blue colors behind the set lit up.

At another show, I was introduced to one of my favorite singers, keyboard player, composer, song writer and record producer Michael McDonald, who was opening for Daryl and John. He was very nice to Charlie and me, and we got to eat with him after soundcheck. He wrote such great songs like, "I Keep Forgettin," "What a Fool Believes," On My Own," "Takin it to the Streets" and many others. He is a great example of a humble man with talent I greatly admire.

My last memory at this point was going to an award show that Hall and Oates performed in New York and, as usual, I would hang backstage. You can see why this book is titled appropriately for the experiences I encountered over the years.

I did see Todd Rundgren backstage and, over the years, we would run into him, especially when he opened for Daryl and John. I liked his music, and our close friend, Eddie, got to play drums for him. I mentioned Eddie earlier in the book.

I was given a ticket to sit in the audience for one of those long award shows with plenty of celebrities surrounding me.

I particularly remember the wonderful duo, Ashford and Simpson, sitting across from me. They were a husband and wife songwriting team and recording artists. I thought it was very romantic working together to make music. I am sure it was not easy at times. The reason I mentioned them was because I was getting really tired sitting, and my feet were killing me. I hated wearing heels, so I took them off, looked around me and across the aisle to see if anybody noticed. Ashford was looking at me, smiling, and he took his shoes off too. I thought that was awesome.

I hope the reader will see from my point of view and understand that there were some amazing musicians that back-up the main performers, but you would not usually recognize their names. I wanted to mention some musicians that I know and really enjoyed being with over the years. They are such talented players and they make the main artists sound even better.

T-Bone Wolk, who played rhythm guitar and was the band director for Daryl and John for many years and also performed with other great artists. Sadly, T-Bone passed away. He is surely missed.

Mickey Curry, drummer; Kasim Sultan on guitar; Paul Pesco, guitarist who use to tour with Madonna. He would start singing the Tommy Roe song, "Sheila," as soon as I would get on the tour bus. I liked Paul, Roger Pope, Caleb Quay [who worked with Elton John], Michael Braun [drummer for Hall and Oates], the Monkees, Foghat and other bands, Eileen Ivers [violinist for Daryl and John and River Dance Show], Stephen Dees [guitarist for Hall and Oates], Victor Wainwright [great blues singer, songwriter and piano player], Greg Kimple [drummer for the band Fantasy, Hall and Oates and other bands], Eliot Lewis [piano, guitar], Brian Dunne [drummer], Klyde Jones [bass], Porter Carroll Jr [percussion and vocals who were all part of The Average White Band, before playing with Daryl and John], Bob Mayo [keyboardist with Peter Frampton, Brian Adams, Hall and Oates. Sadly, Bob passed away while on tour with Brian Adams], Jeff Levine [keyboard who played with Daryl and John, Joe Cocker and the Chamber Brothers], Everett Bradley [singer, songwriter, actor, dancer choreographer, performing with Bruce Springsteen, Bon Jovi, Hall and Oates. We used to hang out at the hotel pool and one-time Everett was being funny and threw me across the pool]. The list goes on, but the guys were always nice to me. It was a joy to hear their stories over the years.

I remember when we toured Sidney, Australia, Jeff Levine [who was playing with Daryl and John] took Charlie and me out for our anniversary to a great vegetarian restaurant. He was so nice to treat us to a fabulous dinner.

Mother's Day 1988

I also wanted to mention John Scarpulla, saxophonist, arranger, composer who we met on Long Island. He had a recording studio and he used to play with Billy Joel, Tower of Power, Hall and Oates, Celine Dion, Mariah Carey, Jennifer Lopez, Michael Bolton and others. We would visit him at his home with his wife in Oyster Bay.

The last musician I would like to acknowledge is Joe Bolero, who plays saxophone at Universal studios with the Blues Brother's Band. Joe and his wife, Yvonne, are wonderful people that we love to connect with sometimes when we have time to see them.

There are so many other musicians Charlie has played with that I can't list them all, so please forgive me if I forgot to list your names.

I also have to recognize Daryl Hall for his talented songwriting and singing. I was indirectly connected to him for over 40 years. Once in a while, when I am walking backstage to meet up with Charlie, Daryl would walk by and surprise me when he would say, "Hello, Sheila," and sometimes with a not-so-often smile. Sorry to say we did not know each other that well, but he does help pay the bills, so I can't complain the way he decided to distance himself. I never did understand why he would not want to hang out with the group sometimes, but I guess it is a role he plays as the employer.

But John is quite different then Daryl. He is a lot more connected to the band and their families that come on the road sometimes. His wife, Aimee, is great. I guess you could say we are "on the road friends" and, once in a while, we text to see how each of us are doing.

I always felt John was not given enough recognition for being an important part of the success of Hall and Oates. Yet he wrote quite a few Hall and Oates songs and eventually became successful as a solo artist and an author. I have to smile when I say John knows me, and it was an honor to get to know his family over the years, too. On rare occasions, we got to hang out with John and go for dinner with him after a show.

I also recall being in Sidney, Australia. Charlie and I went with John and his family to the Taranga Zoo together. Also, years later in Florida, Aimee and I talked John into going with us to the beach. He does not like the beach, but I think he seemed to like hanging with us for a little bit. As far as celebrities go, John gets a thumbs up from me. I think he knows by now that I don't care who you are, but, rather, the kind of person you are that gets me to like someone. It was always a treat backstage to see his mom, dad, and sister, Diane. They always seem glad to see me. One time in Vegas on New Years Eve, I got to sit with his dad to celebrate.

A funny little story about John and his new book, "Change of Seasons," which I enjoyed a lot and got to know him better through his writings [hopefully, he will get to read this book one day]:

John signed and gave Charlie his book, but I wanted him to sign it to me, too. Well, he did, and the story goes like this. I used to pronounce the word Amish with the "ae" sound, and John corrected me. So he signed in his book that I should not forget it is Amish with the "ah" sound. Well, I got him back. He signed my name wrong on the book and put "Shelia," not "Sheila." Charlie told him, and I think he came back with the "ugh" sound, which he probably will not remember. That's okay, because now we are even on grammatical corrections. I had a smile on my face and hopefully he did, too.

HE'S THE PIANO MAN

By Sheila Dechant

He's the piano man,
His eyes on the keyboard,
Music coming through his hands.
Just listen to him play
Everyone is pleased
To see the piano man.

A silent man.
Always telling stories
With just two hands.
You can tell when he smiles
He's in his glory
Piano man, sing your story

Gracious people he will say
I hope you will listen well.
My stories of life, it's hard to see
It's my hands that know it well

So next time you see
Him play his music
Don't ask him questions please
The answers are there loud and clear
You will hear them through the keys.

Journal

March 1989

My goodness, it's been two years since I last wrote in my journal. Nothing really eventful or, thankfully, tragic has happened, except that my brother had to have his eye taken out because he was diagnosed with eye cancer. But he is doing fine.

We got a dog named Bear, and he was a Pomeranian. He turned out to be destructive and would bite too much, so we gave him up and found Sara at the pound. She turned out to be a very sweet dog, and right now she is eight-months-old.

At this time, Jennifer is nine-years-old and April is five. They are doing really well and getting along better. Jennifer is having trouble with social studies, but she started learning to play the flute and seems to like it. April is in ballet and looking beautiful. Her first recital is the day before my 40th birthday.

Charlie and I decided to move back to Florida. We updated our house with new siding and redid the bathroom and the girls' rooms so the house would sell better.

Charlie and I are doing well now, and next Tuesday is our 13th wedding anniversary. Wow! Time sure does go fast. We went out to dinner, and then Charlie played in this band to showcase their music -- mostly for showing groups of people how they sound, especially for weddings.

I finally put an ad in the paper to sell the house. I guess we will just have to wait and see.

Journal

July 30, 1990

It's been a year and we are still on Long Island. The housing market to sell was so bad that it is a waiting game for now.

Last month, Charlie went back on the road with Daryl and John.

Charlie got me a singing machine so I could start working on vocals again, but it didn't work too well. We ended up returning it.

The girls spent a lot of time at the library, especially learning sign language. The teacher taught them sign language by learning songs through music. I thought that was a great idea, and later they got to perform in the city in a group setting.

They also started swimming classes and ceramics classes.

We are now planning our big cruise on October 27, 1990, on the USS Norway. This ship had quite a history that I learned about while writing this book.

USS NORWAY

I was always fascinated by the huge cruise ships since I was little. I want to share some information of one of my most memorable cruise ships that left a lasting impression on me. I hope you find this interesting like I did.

This ship was originally known as the SS France, which was a France ocean liner that was sailing transatlantic crossings from 1961 to 1974. She became the flagship for Norwegian Cruise Line from 1980 to 1999, where her name was changed to the SS Norway. She was the longest passenger ship ever built at that time, until the construction of the Queen Mary Two in the year 2005. What was special about her at that time was her capacity of carrying 8,000 tons of fuel to handle the crossings from Europe to New York. President De Gaulle and his wife were there for the launch and, after cruising trials, she set sail to New York from France in 1961 with famous aristocrats and stars on board. She even had the Mona Lisa on board to New York for touring this famous art work.

In 1973, there was an oil crisis and the development of the Concorde flights which led to no money to operate the SS France anymore, so it was decided it had to stop service. The French union was very angry and they came back on the ship to Le Havre and had over 1,200 passengers taken by ferry back to shore. The crew demanded that they wanted to keep the ship in service, but in the long run, they did not win. And so the ship, in 1974, ended up in Le Havre after 377 crossings and 93 cruises, plus a few world cruises.

Thankfully, the ship was rescued by Oslo, Norway and was rechristened in 1980 with the only ship given permission to fly the United Nation flag as a sign that the ship would have an international crew. She started her maiden voyage to Miami. The ship was so popular that it was more important to be on the ship then the destinations, with added private veranda cabins, new decks [which helped make sure there was enough money to keep her going] but as competition for building bigger and bigger ships even with all the upgrade, she no longer could compete. Eventually, tragedy struck the Norway when a turbo-charged fire erupted on a transatlantic voyage to Barcelona in 1999. They were able to repair her and she sailed, making travel on her very inexpensive from Miami. The ship started to develop mechanical problems and the ship structure was getting worse.

It was around this time that our family was able to go on the Norway for a week. Just walking the decks was so inspiring. The artwork, beautiful architecture and how big she was. I remember just staring out to sea and then looking at her from the decks. First time for us on this mega ship and it left an impression you can't describe.

In 2003, she docked in Miami and there was a boiler explosion, killing seven crew members and injuring 17 as the steam flooded the boiler room, causing a blast into the crew quarters. Luckily, there were no passenger causalities or injuries on board. The end of the majestic Norway was when she went to Germany and a new boiler could not be constructed and, later, large amounts of asbestos were found aboard the ship. Because of the asbestos, the hardest part was where she should be towed and what would happen to all the artwork, library, dining room dishes and other precious artifacts aboard the ship. Just sinking her would cause issues because of the asbestos.

Eventually most of the artifacts were sold to various buyers, including auctioneers and a French museum. There were a lot of rules and regulations on what to do with the remainder of the Norway and this had to be done in accordance to the Basel Convention. There were so many legal problems and the ship was sold. It was the Supreme Court of India that wanted to make sure the ship containing asbestos complied to decontamination before she could be allowed entry in Indian Waters. The ship, as of today, is known as the Blue Lady and is sitting on the muds of Alang, which is a town in the Indian state of Gujarat, where their beaches have become a major world-wide center for ships. It was also known as the graveyard for all ships.

The Supreme Court of India ruled that the beaching of the vessel was in contempt of the courts and therefore illegal. It was a sad ending to a great cruise liner.

Journal 1991

Jennifer was losing her big teeth now. This last tooth is giving her a hard

time, poor thing, it hurts.

We are trying to breed Kasey, our West Highland Terrier, but it's still too early for her to breed.

Charlie's mom and dad were really ill this year. Charlie's dad was having stomach issues and, sadly, his Mom [who we called Nana] developed colon cancer.

We are going to Florida August 9th to help out and visit Miami.

My nephew, David, is coming in August to see us and my friend, Pam. We are all going to see Howie Mandel perform. He is funny.

I got Jennifer signed up to be part of a children's beauty pageant in Cherry Hill, New Jersey. I got her this beautiful gown. She looked so beautiful. She is growing up too fast. She did a wonderful job and did a song in sign language for the talent part, and received a trophy.

April is getting prettier and prettier, and she loves to draw. She was so talented for her age. She wouldn't do stick figures, but, for example, she would draw a clown with such detail. I realized she had a gift.

January 10, 1993

I can't believe it has been two years since I opened my diary to write again. So many things have happened. I hadn't done much, except substitute teach and practice my vocals, working on some of my songs again. I was becoming increasingly unhappy with New York and Charlie. I decided to sell the house as soon as possible. Charlie was hesitant to make a change, but it was just getting too expensive to live here any more and we were just squeezing by financially.

We took another trip to Orlando and we definitely decided to move there. We had a real estate agent set us up in a hotel for a few days to look at different areas to live in, with hopes of better jobs for Charlie while he is off tour, and some opportunities for me, too, hopefully.

Orlando is very big with so many different areas to choose from. I didn't want to live too close to Disney and I wanted to be near good schools for the girls. We found a community in a suburban area that seemed safe, clean and also near the airport for Charlie when he travels.

We decided on a community called Waterford Lakes, and found a subdivision called the Woodlands and put a deposit on a quarter-acre lot to build a ranch style house with four bedrooms on one side and a master bedroom on the other side, with a huge kitchen. Of course, in Florida, you need a pool -- especially for resell purposes. Later on, we wished we hadn't built the pool. We didn't realize how expensive the upkeep was. The land was pie shaped. The girls each had their own bathrooms. The house was not too big, but comfortable, and it reminded me of our house in Centereach, minus the full basement.

We sold our house in Centereach very quickly to a lovely couple. We had a goodbye party with all of our neighbors on Long Island and we took a picture with the new owners of the house before we left. It was bittersweet because there were a lot of good memories of the community and the wonderful neighbors who were our friends, too. They all made us feel welcome. After 10 years we had to say goodbye. Not knowing what would happen next. Did I do the right thing? Time will tell.

One thing that I do regret is when we were packing, I found some leftover stage set items that were used on a video of Hall and Oates for the song "Adult Education. We just had no room for it, and left them behind.

We left Long Island with a U-Haul truck that Charlie was driving. I was driving our van packed with kids, dogs and suitcases. We had gotten on the Long Island Expressway and Charlie was getting into the middle lane ahead of me, when I noticed this car moving right into the lane Charlie was in and almost hit him. Boy, was that scary. Thankfully, he missed the truck. What a way to start our new journey.

Thank goodness, the trip was uneventful, except for the near car accident when we first started. Everybody who travels to Florida or other areas south always have to stop at South of the Border, which was the halfway point to Florida. It is an attraction on interstate 95 and US Highway 301 in Dillon, South Carolina, south of Rowland, North Carolina. South of the Border was south between North Carolina and South Carolina. It is a funky style amusement park and restaurant with touristy shops and firework for sale. When you make it to South of the Border from the New York area, it's the perfect place to take a travel break. The kids loved the chance to get out and run around, eat, and give the dogs a needed walk too.

While our house was being built, we stayed in an apartment called Cypress Run for two months. It was about 15 minutes from our future home. I would commute the kids to school every day, since we were not in the school district at this point. We watched our house being built and got more excited every day.

It was during this time that Hurricane Andrew became a Category five and hit Miami, August 24, 1992. It was the most destructive and costliest hurricane to land in Miami at that time until Katrina in 2005. The brunt of Andrew landed not directly on the coast but paved its way across South Miami, Cutler Ridge into Homestead causing major flooding. It was also the area my sister and brother were living at that time. Hurricane Andrew damaged more than 124,000 homes, including my sister and brother's house. More than 65 people were killed from the storm. There was a lot of flooding issues that took years to repair.

My mother was living in Miami Beach at that time and my sister tried to talk my mother into coming where they were. It never crossed their minds that the Hurricane's force went into the center of Miami and didn't directly hit the Beach side.

Charlie and I came down, bringing supplies and water after Andrew left the area. We saw such devastation near the places I grew up in. Hard to explain if you weren't there. I remember my brother telling me that they had to brace the door with their legs to keep the door from blowing open.

I remember going to my brother's house and looking out to see an apartment across the lake with all the rooms exposed and people standing in their rooms looking down. The whole front of the apartment was gone, so everyone was exposed. Right behind my brother's house was a giant tree with this massive trunk completely torn from the ground.

I heard that a community across from Homestead Air Force Base, where Charlie and I were thinking of moving to before we left for New York, was completely destroyed.

Waiting for insurance people to come and the emotional toll it took was very exhausting. This was also the time Charlie and I were scheduled to leave on a cruise out of Miami. Talk about timing.

Instead of waiting for the electricity to come back on, and who knows when the insurance adjusters would come, my sister and Mom decided to come with us on the cruise, which really helped them get away for a short time.

At least on the cruise, I won a hundred quarters on the slot machine. Charlie and I won a Rock and Roll trivia contest. We even sang and lip synched the song, "My Boyfriend's Back," at Karaoke night and Charlie hates Karaoke -- but it was fun anyways.

When we got back from the cruise, we also had to deal with the fact that my brother was fighting cancer and it was now spreading to his liver. He ended up staying at my sister's house while my sister-in-law had to deal with the repairs on the house.

Charlie and I had to go back home after the cruise because I had applied for a position with Disney World. I didn't want to leave everyone, but now it was up to the insurance companies, which could take months to solve, and there was nothing more we could do to help for now.

Finally, on Halloween, the house was ready and we were finally home. We have adjusted pretty well and getting everything unpacked was another hurdle we had to complete, which we did in a few weeks.

I was persistent with running to the casting office to get any kind of position at Disney and, finally, November 19th, I was hired and my training began. Unfortunately, the company really didn't care what kind of degree or training you had. Everyone had to start at the bottom unless you knew someone already working there. All employees were called cast members.

Disney did make training fun, I must admit, with lots of awards for completing each class. They finally gave me my position in merchandise working for different areas of MGM studios, which is now known as Hollywood Studios.

I had different roles as a cashier, stocking and helping customers in different areas of the park. For   instance, I had to dress up in an orange star tours costume to work at Star Tours. I felt silly wearing the costume, but it was a job. I also worked for the Villain Store and the News stand, which no longer exists at the parks today. The worst part of the job was not only the pay, but the hours. You had no choice but to work evenings, weekends and holidays, but I figured if I was there for a while, the hours would get better.

A short time after I started, I had an accident.

It was around Christmas time. I was at the backstage area going to get my paycheck and to start my shift at Star Tours. I stepped down from the sidewalk to the street, and there was a large drainage area that you can't see from the sidewalk. I fell down right where the street and the drainage slanted. I fell and could hardly stand back up . A cast member told me to go into the employee lounge area. I barely could walk, as something was wrong with my left ankle. I limped to the lounge and a guard came over and said I would have to get to the onsite clinic. He just left leaving me there basically to fend for myself.

In the middle of the holiday crowd and still in my orange costume I limped to the clinic in pain and they told me I had to get to my car and go to the off-site emergency care, off property. Going through the large crowds again, in my mind, I knew this was just making my ankle worse.

After I was examined, the doctor told me that my ankle ligaments were torn but not broken. I ended up on medical leave, but you have to be careful, especially when you first start working. You don't want Disney corporation to think I was trying to get money out of them, which some people would do. Soon after, I went back to work with using crutches. What a way to start a new job.

Working at Star Tours was fun, especially watching people get off the ride. One day, who comes walking into the store but Steven Spielberg himself. Years later, I ran into him backstage at the Rock and Roll Hall of Fame.

While this was going on, my brother was becoming critical and he flew to Dana Farber Cancer Institute to see if they could help him. There, he would be closer to his kids, Marilyn and Robert.

I ended up asking Disney if I could take time off to be with my brother in Boston, so they let me go.

I walked into my brother's room and I felt strange seeing him there with his face drawn and thin. It was a rough time for everyone. It got really bad, but the doctor said, "your brother is unique and is fighting this disease." His mind was not working sometimes, and he had short-term memory loss. My brother's main problem was his white cells were off the charts. My brother did beat the odds this time, and they got his white cells under control and he was able to go back home. He was almost near death and pulled through, but no one knew how long he had, since the cancer was spreading.

I worked at Disney and was promoted to a position called Research and Statistics, where you stand outside asking guests about where they live, how many were in their family, why they are here, etc. The pay was minimum wage and not great at all. They finally offered me a job working for their insurance company, which was an air-conditioned trailer in the back lot of MGM. This job was quite interesting for a while. In the trailer were computers. We can see people on the monitors coming off the Star Tours ride and the people would come up to the Kiosk and see me. My job was to ask them if they have a family member who may have taken out an insurance policy, but for some reason never told anyone. I had to ask questions to see if their name was showing up. Truthfully, I thought this was almost impossible, but you never know. One time, a lady came up to the kiosk and she told me her last name was Hines. It turned out she was the wife of the famous tap dancer, Gregory Hines. She was so nice and I was so thrilled to be talking to her. She looked right at me and whispered, "don't tell anyone," and she winked at me.

Gregory Hines was one of my idols and a great American actor, singer and choreographer who died of cancer at age 57. I remember seeing him in a movie with Mikhail Baryshnikov called "White Knights." Mikhail was also an amazing classical dancer who was born Russian and became and American dancer, choreographer and actor.

Another once-in-a-lifetime moment was when I was eating at the Disney employee cafeteria and, all of a sudden, everyone stopped talking. I looked up, and there was Princess Diana coming through as a way to be not seen with her family so she could go to the rides with her children. I did get to see her for a brief moment.

While working at the insurance company with some wonderful cast members, we found out awhile later that after we were hired, we were demoted, losing six-month seniority. They had said we were promoted to working for both the insurance company and still be employed by Disney Corporation.

That was so confusing and was quite unfair, especially not being told until after we took this position.

My co-worker friend was so mad that she went directly to the chairman and chief executive of Walt Disney Company to complain of the unfairness. Weeks later, she had left this job and started her own wedding planning business.

Eventually I tried for a position as a cruise agent for the company. Since I had trouble with one test and they would not let me repeat the test again, I left the company.

After Disney World, I got a position as concierge with the Peabody Hotel in Orlando.

The main Peabody hotel was built in Memphis in the 1930's, and the then another Peabody Hotel was built in Orlando in 1986, but was later purchased by the Hyatt Regency in 2013.

The general manager of the time, Frank Schutt, had returned from a hunting trip. He and his friends had a lot of fun with leaving duck decoys in the hotel fountain. Everyone loved the idea, and since then, both hotels used five Mallard ducks, one male and four females, to march from their home -- which was on the top of the hotel with a beautiful enclosure for them. Every day at 11:00 a.m., the Duck Master would escort the ducks to the elevator with the music of, "King Cotton March," by John Phillip Sousa. The ducks entered the lobby where they waddled onto a long red carpet that led them to a fountain made of solid Italian marble. The concierge desk was right near the fountain, so we saw the parade every day. At exactly 5 p.m. the ducks would follow the duck master back onto the red carpet and go back to the elevator to their enclosure.

The duck master's position came about in 1940, when a bellman by the name of Edward Pembroke, who was a former circus animal trainer, volunteered to care for the ducks. He trained them to march into the hotel lobby which is famously known as the "Duck March."

Over time, the ducks became very famous with an appearance on "The Tonight Show," when Johnny Carson was the host. They were also on Sesame Street, The Oprah Winfrey Show, and even an article was written on them in

People magazine.

They even had honorary duck masters who were guests, like Patrick Swayze, Oprah Winfrey, Kevin Bacon, etc.

Occasionally, while I was working, one of the ducks got out of the fountain, and I would get one or two back into the water. There were times Mark, the duck master who spoke five languages, would take them to a hotel room for a bath. It was quite a sight.

The concierge position was a really great job, but I hated the wool jacket and skirt we had to wear. It didn't make sense to me when we were living in Florida, but I guess it was tradition. I worked in the lobby and helped the guests to make dinner reservations and to find any information they may need. I met some fascinating people, like Walter Cronkite, famous musicians and politicians. I always felt they were just regular people who did something special, or who knew the right people to boost their career at the right time.

I also worked upstairs on the 26th floor, which was mainly for the V.I.P's with an amazing view of Orlando. I remember one time I was working at night and got to see the space shuttle crossing over the moon. I was so mad that I didn't have my camera that night. It was breathtaking.

On this hotel level, we were licensed to serve and sell liquor and expensive food to the guest for breakfast, and appetizers like shrimp in the early evenings.

I had one bad experience while I was working.

All employees received free meals at the employee cafeteria, which was very good ... until one day I came home really sick to my stomach. I ended up going to the emergency room with agonizing pain. It turned out I had gotten food poisoning. I think it was because the buffet-type meals were not kept hot enough and, later, I heard the food was also leftovers from catering, but I am not sure if that was true or not. I was pretty scared in the hospital, and having IV's to keep me hydrated resulted in my veins collapsing. So nurses were having a hard time finding a vain. After a few days, I was able to go home and then back to work.

I stayed at the Peabody for almost four years. I left because of the long hours and working weekends and no choice on days you had to work. It was getting hard for the girls, and I had a chance to go with Charlie to Hawaii, and they wouldn't let me take the time off.

Years later, the Peabody in Orlando was sold and became the Hyatt. That must have been sad for all the employees who had to say goodbye to a prestigious hotel.

SHEILA'S SONG

By Sheila DeChant

Sheila sat upon a hill
And thought about her days
Why she chose the road she did
What made her feel very sad?
Thinking about her dad
Who's gone and won't come back

Music was her life she knew
But could not find her place
Family did not believe in her
She had to find her way
She met a man playing in a band
He had a dream. She believed in him
It's Sheila's story
She smiles and cries
Made of Love and glories
Going through her life

Sheila knows her youth has past
But still her dreams are strong
To be remembered well
To finally hear her songs
It makes her feel that it's worth the wait.
To leave a piece of her behind
Even when she is gone.

August 1996

After I came back from Hawaii, I was searching for a new job. I started feeling creative again and composed a song called, "Palermo." Charlie worked on it with me by arranging and writing it out. I was so pleased we finally worked together. It made me really happy. At 47, it felt like a big weight was off my shoulders. Even with doubts I had about my music abilities. I knew there was something there. The melodies were in my head, but I had never followed my heart until now.

Meanwhile, my girls are getting big and into the teenage years. I didn't have a lot of problems with Jennifer as a teenager except the usual "I am going to my friend's house," knowing that is not all they were doing. I knew I had to let her go little by little. She had such a sensitive soul, and I worried because she gets hurt so easily. She did have one serious situation that happened, but let's say she learned her lesson. Charlie and I supported her, and she showed her strength in so many ways and was able to move forward to a wonderful life.

Then it was April's turn to start the teenage years. She definitely had her own way of dealing with the emotional highs and lows, and she was growing so fast. It finally happened sadly, but it was expected that she did not want me to hold or kiss her anymore. I felt like I was now the enemy, but I tried to convince myself that her problems would eventually get better with time. Her artwork always surprised and impressed me. Her drawings were special, and I hope she will always keep art an important part of her life.

Well, I am pursuing a career in travel and I hope it will work out for me. I still love composing songs and I hope Charlie and I can continue to do so. I was so happy that we finally got "Palermo" recorded. That was such a rush when I heard it being played for the first time with a band. It's a feeling you can't describe. Now I understand how it feels when a group of notes you assembled create a melody you hear as you play. It feels awfully good when it is completed, played and recorded.

August 1997

It seems like yesterday I wrote in this book, yet a year has passed. I am in my bedroom and I am depressed. My daughters are in the full teenage years of 17 and 14 and I have become a terrible mother, at least according to my daughters. I was so hoping that they would want to be loving and caring to their mom, but raging teenage hormones take over, and now I feel more alone then ever. This time in their lives can be very hard on parents. The icing on the cake is being told by my doctor that I am going through menopause and I have to take hormone pills. That is why it is called the change. You never know if taking these pills is good or bad for you, so I keep reading articles about different ways to handle menopause. This was a hard time for me.

I traveled a lot for the first time this summer. We took April on a trip out west to Phoenix, Grand Canyon, Sedona, Vegas, L.A. and Santa Anna. I hope April did get some benefit from the trip. It was difficult to tell. This was the first time I left Jennifer, but she did well, especially with her boyfriend, Jon, who she met in high school band. I was just concerned that she was becoming too dependent on Jon. I am hoping she will develop some inner strength and will understand herself better.

I went without Jennifer and April on tour with Charlie to Long Island, Boston and Baltimore. I just felt this was my time to leave without pressure. We had a wonderful time. It was a first for Charlie and me without the girls.

The last day on this tour went badly, though. Everyone in the organization must have been upset or something, and I felt like an unwelcomed visitor. I got very uncomfortable and I wanted to jump off the tour bus and fly home.

I really did like Rick, the bus driver; Paul, the guitar player; Bob May; and John Oates. I felt comfortable with them and I loved more of their stories and experiences which was mostly about music. I was glad to get back to the hotel room.

My music is so important to me. I started to get bored and envious, and was definitely excluded on the tours. I was caught between just staying home alone or start a new life without Charlie. It is Charlie's job, but then again, there is so much down time between shows. He seems glad I am with him most of the time. We are either with each other all the time or not at all.

Tough situation to be in when we care about each other. Taking care of my girls and yet being able to work on my own projects is not easy to do, especially when you see so many musicians getting divorced. Or breaking up.

That, right there, was the last writings of my journal.

Well, where am I now going on my journey? My girls are pretty self-sufficient and didn't seem to need me anymore or want me with them too much. Now I can concentrate more on where I should go next career wise.

I did substitute teach for a few years. I was able to finally get certified to teach fulltime, but the politics of the school system was really not helping the children to get a good education, with so many obstacles in their way.

For instance, I was called in at the last-minute right before the end of the school year to take over a class because the teacher had been fired. It was a first grade class. I went to the school and walked into the room. There were no lesson plans, books, paper or pencils for the students. It seems the teacher took everything and left the children with nothing.

Here I was, in a classroom of about 25 children that I had to help get through the rest of the year. I finally asked the other teachers how they managed and if they had any materials I could use. I did get a few things and made up lesson plans the best I could. I went home and spent hours figuring out material for the children.

The next step was seeing what these children's needs were. It turned out to be quite a mess. Basically, I could see why the previous teacher walked out. Some of these children needed to be in a special education class and could not handle a regular classroom situation. I think the education department decided these children needed to be mainstreamed, no matter what the situation was. There were children that were working at grade level or higher, but there were children with behavior issues that made it difficult for the children who wanted to learn. I could understand handling one or two children, but there were at least five or six that needed more one-to-one help. Even if you were able to divide the children into groups. I could see that an assistant was warranted in this situation.

I decided since it was so close to the end of the school year, I would do a lesson plan that would keep their interest, no matter what level they were at.

I put together a butterfly project and thank goodness... it was successful.

Meanwhile, I heard that another child in another classroom had run out of the school and disappeared. The next thing we knew, there was a search party and helicopters looking for the child, who was eventually found unharmed.

Another classroom situation I had to deal with was when a child brought in a lighter and hid it in his desk. The next thing I knew, the father comes walking into the classroom, which is not allowed, and started taking the child. I told the father he needed to go to the office for permission because, as a substitute teacher, how would I know if he was the parent. He walked out with the child and I grabbed a teacher to watch my class. I followed the father, who ended up in the office. I was so nervous and responsible for the well-being of the child.

In those days, since you were a substitute teacher, the schools do not protect you if something happens in a classroom, so basically, you're on your own with no help from the county if something happens to the children under your care. Most substitute teachers did not know that.

I came to the conclusion that I loved the children, but I hated how they were being treated. Hopefully, things will get better for them, but it was out of my hands. Since I did not have any seniority, I decided to pursue another career while still trying to compost and also enjoy my other hobby, taking pictures.

This was also when a friend of mine suggested going to travel school because of my prior traveling experiences.

Later I was offered a full-time position teaching, but I decided to try a new venture, instead.

EYES OF THE SOUL

I have always tried to get the camera to catch what I see. I felt that if people looked at my photos, they could connect or understand the feelings I experienced at that moment when I shot the picture. It's just like a musician, performing to people and trying to connect to the audience.

To capture a moment in time that will never come again in the same way. It is as close as any person can get to the inside of their soul, I felt.

Sometimes, I can't help but watch life in frames. For instance, sitting in my living room and watching my 16-year-old daughter, April, reading her school books while I have a picture in my mind of her doing the same thing when she was 10. This gives me a strong sense of time moving forward. As I get older, I start feeling the moments as very precious, but fleeting. It is moving forward way too fast. That is when pictures become part of one's soul and makes time stand still for an instant.

My daughter never understood the concept of why I took so many pictures. She often got upset with me for taking shots of her at different times of her life. I guess that, in my heart, I was holding on to her youth and those special moments, but she felt that I was intruding on her life, instead. Later on, she also became a really good photographer. She also continued her artistic gift.

I did win a few awards for some pictures I took, but nothing on a grand scale as of yet. Later on, Charlie asked me to do his CD cover, and one of my photos was a shot of Hurricane Charlie coming into Orlando, right over our house. It turned out to be a great photo. I took so many shots as the years passed, but, for one reason or another, I never pursued a career in photography. There were too many people doing the same thing, and you need pictures that would stand out from the masses. I am still working on that.

A memorable moment of taking a picture was when Hall and Oates were playing for the Para-Olympics and I was in the back of the stage. Al Gore was near me, and he asked me to take a picture of him with a disabled violinist. I was surprised he asked me, but it was an honor to do so.

Then, a few minutes later, looking down at the stairs that were in back of the stage, was Liza Minnelli—who, if you don't know, is the daughter of the late Judy Garland, and who also starred on Broadway in the show Cabaret. Her co-star was the famous Broadway dancer, actor and singer, Joel Grey.] I was just remembering that my dad knew his dad because they both came from the same neighborhood in New York City. I just happened to be in the right place and the right time to take a picture of Liza coming up the stairs.

SINGING COMPETITION

I was driving home one day and I saw a store named Sing Along, so I decided to stop by and see what it was about. It turned out to be a Karaoke store with all kinds of backing tracks to song that you can buy, and a night club area in the rear of the store for people to come in and sing Karaoke on the weekends. I bought some backing tracks that I used at home with a microphone and started singing again. It was difficult at first, because a lot of the songs were in a key that didn't fit my voice, so I had to be picky with what I was singing.

Me practicing for Dick Clark's Karaoke Competition.

I would go to the club on the weekends and watch some of the performers. I finally had the nerve to try a few songs on stage. It turned out surprisingly better than I thought. After singing there for a few months, a competition was starting around the country for the Dick Clark American Bandstand Karaoke Competition. I decided to try out. I picked out a song called, "The Mummers Dance," by a Canadian Celtic singer, Loreena McKennitt from "The Book of Secrets." The song was used as the theme for the TV series, "Legacy," and was featured in the film, "Ever After," starring Drew Barrymore. It was the perfect song for my voice and the key was perfect for my voice. I decided to work hard and see for myself if I had any vocal ability.

On the night of the competition, I got up on stage and it felt good for a change. I was there, on my own to see if performing is what I really wanted.

It is hard to follow the lyrics with this kind of competition, but I knew the lyrics really well. I performed listening to the sound of the tracks and blending vocally with each chord, and it felt good. It was a long wait before they announced the winners. I did not win first place, but I did come in third and won a four-song demo.

A few weeks later, I went into the store and recorded four songs. At least I have the demo and I was happy that I did try to sing. I knew I had it in me. I realized that, because of that inner feeling of low self-esteem, I felt that I really liked composing music better than singing. I did not think I had the talent to do stage performing. I also knew with Charlie on the road and the nature of the music business, I had to look for another career. I still held on to music and tried to compose when I could.

I am definitely not Irish but these lyrics just came easy for me for some reason.

AN IRISH PUB

By Sheila Dechant

Driving down Dublin's Highways
Knowing the turmoil is there
I met two people walking
One was Irish and one English was here
I stopped to help their travels
They gladly came right in
We talked of anger brewing
What makes them so sincere?

John said, "They broke the cycle."
In an Irish pub one night
They argued with each other
Tearing at people's broken hearts

John screamed and shot the gun off
The mad crowd stopped and stared
Where you come from doesn't matter

We must all survive here
We must come to an understanding
Shedding blood or loved one's tears
As we all bury others
Let's try to stop it here

You never heard such silence
One man held up his beer
He said, "I'm sick of fighting
Let's end the anger here"
John went on to talk on TV.
No one knows how the feud began
English and Irish hunting
For ways to end more lost sons

Great men and noble sons
Heard the story of the Irish Pub
Told the tale to their children
How the father stopped the guns

THE CRUISING WORLD

My next venture was travel school. I started classes and became friends with Toni Blake, a sweet southern woman with short dark hair, a vibrant personality and full of fun. She also owned part of a recording studio in Texas, and a close friend of hers was best friends with Priscilla Presley.

We completed training and now it was time to look for a job. The travel school was also a cruise company, so I worked there for a little while. I learned how to sell cruises to clients. Basically, we were usually paid strict commission. The pay was not great but it was good experience for me. I ended up going back to substitute teaching until the right cruise job became available.

Toni called me and said she was working for a company and wanted to see if I wanted to start work there, since they were hiring. To me, it was a chance to really settle down with a permanent position, and that is what I did.

Cruise ships fascinated me because of their size and how they could sail on the water without sinking. I also had a curiosity of planes and the way they are held up by the wind. A little scary to me, but the world of cruise ships and the building of different size planes was exciting and I knew little about them -- until I did the training and started working.

Competition in the cruise and travel industry was very limited at first, but people wanted the product and also the best cabin for the least amount of money. The company I worked for was owned by Carnival Cruise line, and was eventually sold quite a few times.

Selling was easy for me since I loved the ships. The hard part was making sure the clients had all the proper documentation or they would not be allowed to board the ships, even after paying the money. Very strict policies are in place, since most of the ships are not registered with the United States.

There were other issues that all passengers need to be aware of, and that's being ready for any problems that could happen, like being sick, missing the cruise because of a plane delay, family emergency at home, documents that don't match the name [like being married and the name wasn't changed], making the cruise line aware if client has a disability or allergies to certain food. So many issues could come up that selling is the easy part, but taking care of the client can result in client being refused boarding.

The commissions we earned were based on how many cabins we sold and the kind of cabin the client wants. It varied depending on what they could afford.

The worst part of the job was missing a lot of family time because the hours were long and included weekends, evenings and holidays.

I did very well and started making big commissions. I was given the opportunity, after a few years, to work at home, and that is what I did. It took some time to the right equipment set up and to connect to the cruise server, but eventually I settled in.

I did surprisingly well and met some amazing people who called me from all over the world. One example was a call from Margaret Disney, who I think was Walt Disney's sister-in-law. I made a friend out of one of my clients, who was a drummer who worked locally in Venice, Florida. He later on got to sing with Todd Rundgren, and we are still friends with his wife today.

My job became the stage, and I was performing, as well as educating, many clients on what to expect on a cruise ship. Many of them had never been on a cruise before, and I gave them the information they needed. Of course, other clients knew exactly what they wanted. I was a sales person who became an educator and a friend on each call.

Orlando is known as the lightning capital of the world. Our storms can be quite scary. Once I was working at home when a storm started. The thunder was loud and, all of a sudden, as I was working, lightning struck right outside my window. It was so loud that the whole room turned white and my head phones sounded like electricity through my ears. I jumped out of my seat and ran into my bedroom shaking like crazy. I knew the lightning must have hit something very near the house. I called the office later to let them know that my phone line is down and that I was not going back on until the storm had passed.

The company was sold again, and this time the news was not good. The industry started changing again, and the competition was getting worse. Instead of caring about the client, it was all about volume, not the safety of the clients. The phones would never stop ringing, and I had to reach a certain quota in order to make good commissions. The situation made working so stressful that after almost 10 years, I decided to retire.

This job had become a career, and I occasionally miss it. However, it made being with Charlie harder and harder. His tour schedule and my long hours were often conflicted. It was time to retire and hopefully compose more songs and, finally, be able to write a book.

TO THE PEOPLE

By Sheila DeChant
See the faces as they go by
You're watching for signs
Of their true feelings inside
I can't understand how they fascinate me
Looking for signs by what they say

Hear the music as they dance to
Sweet sounds of Mitchell
I want to see through their eyes
Today it's the rhythm
That caresses your soul
Maybe it's the time that deadens their spirit
Can you hear it, can you hear it?

Now they just walk by
People start looking the same
What happened to the creative creatures?
Did they all fade, become shy?

To other generations who finally speak up
Will you finally speak up, will you?

THE JOURNEY GOES ON

I have to admit it, I am now 68 years young. My cervical stenosis and low spine issue continue with added arthritis but at least it is not cancer. I can definitely say, "I am a pain in the neck." I am still optimistic about life in general.

Me with my stepsisters, Roberta and Janice.

Amazingly, Charlie is still working at age 75. It is so strange to say we are that age. You always think it is years and years away, and then it's here. People say age is a state of mind and I agree. Anyway, we have no choice, we either don't think about age, or we can go into deep depression. I rather not think about it. My mind says, "it's not true, no way," and then I look in the mirror and Charlie and I think, "who are these people?" When I look at Charlie, I still see the young sparkle of Charlie looking at me sometimes from the stage. Looking back, it surely was romantic.

I am keeping busy shooting pictures of my daily life and special events that happen that I love. As each day passes, I try to hold on to each moment. Either I am sitting down to try and compose, watch my favorite shows on television, do some art, go to family gatherings, or meet with Charlie in different places. I always try to keep busy. I usually meet Charlie during his last few days of a

Me and Charlie, backstage after a show with Daryl Hall & John Oates.

tour so he can fly back with me. I am also making plans to complete a couple of children's books that I worked on throughout the years while watching my family on their journeys. So, you can see we all have different experiences. It's all about dealing with common issues that makes me feel not so alone in this life.

My girls and my grandchildren are successful in their careers and marriages, so thank goodness there is no drama there. Well, maybe there is a little drama, but at the end it works itself out.

Charlie with his Orlando-based band, The Kings. L-R Tommy Calton, James "Cadillac" Cardarelli, Larry Jacoby and Steve Sienkiewicz.

I almost had the opportunity to meet President Obama and Michele Obama when Hall and Oates played for them. It seems that Michele likes them. Unfortunately, it did not happen for me, but something else happen that was almost as good.

Hall and Oates got to play on the Jimmy Fallon show and I got to be in the audience.

Right next to where Jimmy Fallon interview guests, a moving stage came out, left of the The Roots band with Hall and Oates on the stage -- which surprised me, seeing how small the stage was. But overall, the performance was good.

After the show, Jimmy ran up the left side of the audience, shook hands with people and eventually came down the right side where I was. He came by and shook my hand, I told him who I was, and he was so delighted that he shook my hand again with a big smile. He was not the President of the United States but it was still a great experience. He seemed genuinely nice. I liked that about him. Later on, I found out someone had shot the picture of me shaking hands with him, so that was an added bonus.

Our niece, Darlene, and nephew, David.

At the end of 2016, some of the band wives and I were going to Hawaii because Hall and Oates were scheduled to play in Oahu and Maui. Unfortunately, and for a rare occurrence, Daryl got sick and the shows were cancelled. John Oates make it possible for all of us to still go, and we really appreciated him doing that for all of us.

Most significant others don't go to the shows unless they are in the same place for more than two days. Most shows are one-day travel, then show, and then the group leaves right after to go to the next city. Some wives also have jobs or young children. It is not easy, but that's part of the job.

I was not feeling good myself before the trip to Hawaii, but it was such a nice thing for John to do for us. We flew to Oahu and I was miserable on the plane. It was Economy Plus and my seat was hard as a board. It was so long, and then we had to fly in circles for a while before we landed. Afterwards, we had to get a rental car, and when we got on the road to Waikiki it was gridlock traffic. I was about to scream at that point. After a good night's sleep, I was better, but still a little tired.

Our youngest daughter and her husband had lived in Oahu for almost a year, but we never got to see them when they lived there. We rented a car and we got to see where they lived.

Me and my youngest daughter, April.

Later on, we headed toward the north shore to a family-owned 400-acre private nature preserve and cattle ranch, Kualoa Ranch. It is about 24 miles from Honolulu where parts of Jurassic Park were filmed. Charlie and I enjoyed being tourists.

After visiting the ranch, we went further on to the other side of the north shore to see the giant waves. It was rainy and misty, but we did get to see them.

A few days before Halloween, October 2016, a day after the show, we flew from Honolulu to Maui and rented a car at the airport. We drove to the Kea Lani Resort, where we were welcomed at the front desk with drinks and leis. It was a beautiful hotel, and we went right to the pool, where we met up with some of the band members and the road manager.

Since we were there during Halloween, we got to go to the town of Lahaina and see the parade of people in amazing costumes parading down the street. We just sat on a wall to watch, and it was a lot of fun.

We also got to stay a few days with our son-in-law's cousin's house. He works for the parks department and had a beautiful house near Hana Highway. It was quite a treat to see them, and it was nice of them to let us stay with them for a few days. Can you imagine getting up every morning to the views of the mountains and the water? Nice job.

The trip was one of the best we had in a long time, except for getting to Hawaii. I guess it was worth it, though.

After we got back, Charlie got a gig with local artists at the Fontainebleau Hotel on Miami Beach. The reason I mentioned this show and its venue is because I had a flashback of my dad playing there when I was little. It is almost like coming full circle, but it is my husband instead of my dad.

We stayed at my sister's house and, of course, the family met for our favorite barbecue, Shorty's.

I asked my sister if she had any family VHS tapes, and she had three of them. One of them was produced form an old 8mm of our family growing up. It wasn't very good quality, but at least we had some old footage and I was able to have some converted -- not only those tapes to DVD, but others that I had of my immediate family, including the interview Jennifer had with Dick Clark, and the Liberty Concert. If you have never converted any of your old tapes, it is really worth the money to have that done.

I sat down to watch one of the tapes, and I was touched when I realized I did not remember a lot of my childhood. It did look like we were happy together, with my mom dancing with my dad, and even seeing my dad hold my hand and playing music at the beach. It touched my heart and left me somewhat sad to see all the fleeting moments that will never come back. I guess that is why I keep taking pictures, to hold onto what passes in our lives so quickly.

April wrote the family a beautiful letter that showed how similar our journeys are.

To My family

About a year ago today, Robert and I set off on our dream to live in different places and experience life as travelers. We've experienced many wonderful things in such a short time, made some serious lifelong memories and met some great people along the way. We planned the trip the best we could but found, like most things planned in life that we have no idea about, we were mostly required to fly by the seat of our pants. There were three lessons we learned out here on our travels.

Lesson #1: The importance of Family

You may be asking yourself, "How could one travel 4,644 miles away to learn the importance of family? Well, I'm here to inform you that one needs to be apart in order to appreciate. I found that we miss everyone, but that couldn't happen if we were within arm's reach since, as they saying goes, "distance makes the heart grow fonder."

Lesson #2: The perks and disadvantages of being a traveler.

We came so close to not even doing this experience. We were blessed with the opportunity to travel through 11 states this year and to experience the desert, glaciers and mountains. Looking back, I wish I could've done it earlier in life, which proves that Europeans need a year break before college for traveling. There are, of course, the disadvantages of traveling, e.g. dealing with constant change, never having a place to call you own and, worst of all, bed bugs!

Finally, Lesson #3

Traveling brings you to some amazing places but... The more amazing the place is, the more crowded and expensive it is. The less populated places are slower-paced, but limit your accessibility to stores and such. Every place has a decent amount of annoying people who make you grumble about how much you absolutely hate tourists, until you realize that you also, in fact, are a tourist. Nowhere is the perfect place to live. Hawaii is great and all, but there is one thing Hawaii doesn't have, and it's all of you.

In conclusion, when the holidays come around the corner, we begin to think of our family traditions, meals at Linda and Ed's big wooden table, and watching the kids play. We miss the guys wandering off to catch fish, hanging out at the pool, quiet kitchen counter conversations while drinking something delicious, Jon horrifying me shooting fireworks under my chair. All of those little things add up to what we are missing out here and make us appreciate all of you more.

And now, a toast: Please hold up your drink, be it milk, beer or wine or all three. Here's to family, to love, to each other. Life is too short, so don't forget to enjoy the little things, cherish the moments and laugh together. Drink, eat and be merry. Cheers!

Love, April and Robert

I really loved that letter she wrote. I was very proud of her bravery to take such a trip far away from family and friends. Part of me always tensed up a little, waiting for a phone call that sometime happened, all the while hoping she was alright. It turned out, she was.

Friends and family.

FINALE

I am sitting at my desk in my bedroom realizing that I have come to the end of my story, and I really did not want to end my book yet. So many things to remember and so many things I probably forgot.

We just got back from a trip to Savannah, Georgia to watch our grandson, Dylan, who is now two while April and our son-in-law, Robert, went to a wedding. We really loved Savannah and the famous River Walk. The fish was fresh and the atmosphere felt a little like St. Augustine and New Orleans to me, but it felt a little more peaceful as you take a walk along the River. The beautiful old homes and lovely parks made this a great trip.

Our daughters, Jennifer & April

My long relationship with Charlie, aging, physical change and different ways of looking at life at this point is challenging, but we still have this strong connection that was with us since the first day we met. The feelings are still there, and with a twinkle in his eyes and an extra flutter in my heart ... but then I just want to run away from the whole situation.

My journey continues and I must admit, music gets us through a lot of hard times that make us stronger and more committed.

If you ask me if it was all worth it, my reply most likely would be mixed. Sometimes I wouldn't give up this way of life, but other times, I wonder what it would be like to be married to someone who comes home every day. Who knows, I could also be bored in that scenario, too.

And more fun with more friends & family.

If you believe in horoscopes, I am a Gemini, as is Charlie and our youngest daughter, April [but Jennifer is a Libra]. I do see where there are really seven people in our family sometimes. Our personalities change sometimes, like we are different people, except for Jennifer.

I will continue to write and hopefully start composing, but I won't be singing any more. One of these days, you will probably see me on one of the Hall and Oates shows just hanging around. I don't mind saying hello to people. I am usually on the side of the stage, wandering behind the curtains or walking through the audience to get that adrenaline feel before the show. I can't wait to see my book completed. What a thrill for me that people will hopefully care about a girl who grew up in Florida, and will care about the adventure I took.

Thank goodness I still love to write and shoot pictures. It keeps me alive in some ways. I am eternally grateful for what I have achieved, and all the wonderful families, friends and acquaintances I have met.

I also have some good news and some bad news to share. I will start with the bad news first.

The end of October 2018, our dog of 18 years, Kayla, started having problems walking. One night, Charlie and I hear her yelping continuously in pain that seemed to last forever. It was heart-wrenching to hear. The pain was so bad we couldn't lift her without causing more pain. We went to the vet and

Our last dog, Kip, at 14.

they said it was her nerves being pinched near her spinal cord. They said it was getting worse. A few days went by and she seemed herself again, but that was not for long.

At the same time, we received sad news that our good friend, Eddie, who I wrote about early on, had suddenly passed away.

We left Kayla at home. The pet sitter would come in two times a day to check in on her so that we could go down to Miami for the viewing and funeral for Eddie.

We were at the viewing and we got to see some dear friends that we hadn't seen in years. We got a call from the sitter that Kayla could not walk anymore. We called our next-door neighbor to keep checking on her, but Charlie and I decided to drive right back, which takes about four hours from Miami. We walked into the house from the garage and Kayla was sprawled on the floor near her bowl. We knew it was time to say goodbye to her. That same morning, we took her to the vet and she went peacefully. That was very hard because she was with me when the girls had just left home.

A week later, on November 4, Charlie was on tour again and I took our other dog of 16 years, Kip, to our community dog park. We got back into the car, but before I drove off, I noticed a rainbow appear and it started to rain.

I was finishing a children's story and, seeing the view of the rain and the rainbow, I quickly grabbed my camera. I had thought I had put my car's gear into park, so I quickly stepped one foot out of the car to avoid getting the camera wet, to shoot what I saw outside the car – a picture of the rainbow for my book. My car started moving backwards.

The family eating at the Cracker Barrel.

I tried grabbing the gear but I couldn't reach it. The car kept moving backwards, and I fell to the ground. I tried reaching with my right hand to the brake while looking back at Kip, who was in the back seat. I was so worried about him. The car suddenly turned and the next thing I knew, the front tire rolled onto my left side and stopped on top of my upper thigh and I was pinned down. The pain I felt, I can't describe. I tried pulling myself out, but I was trapped. Screaming at the top of my lungs [which seemed like forever], some man saw me from the road. He drove the car off of me. I must have been in shock because I got up. He asked if he should call 9-1-1, but I said I had to get my dog home. I drove back and called my son-in-law's dad, who lives close to me. He took me to the emergency room.

Me and Charlie with John Oates and friends Linda and Ed.

I was given morphine. Diagnosis was muscle trauma, numbness left side of my leg, meniscus tear, left knee, slap tear of my left shoulder. Thank God, somehow no broken bones from the pressure of the tire landing on my leg, which saved me from the car going further and causing more damage.

With all of these situations happening at once, I know I developed PTSD and depression. But with counseling and physical therapy, it is true, that time starts healing the wounds. I still have shoulder, neck and knee issues, but I am not willing yet to agree on surgery. Luckily, the auto insurance company called it an accident and covered most of my medical care.

Our grandchildren & grandnieces.

So now the good times roll, finally.

I turned 70 years old and we celebrated with family and friends on Amelia Island, hosted by my daughters. It was a wonderful weekend of just relaxing, swimming, going to the beach, and, of course, eating. My daughters made this cake out of lottery tickets. I thought that was quite unique, and I loved it.

Now I have at least four of my songs on Charlie's CD, so that was very special to me.

One day, some young woman came to my front door. She was working for an Investment company and asked me what our financial goals were. I talked

Charlie's sister, Janine, and nephews Josh and Chad.

to her a little about being in the music field, and she said she may have someone that could help us with furthering Charlie's career of promoting his own music, and help with promoting my book and my children's stories.

Our 4th grandchild, Julian.

The woman called me and gave me a name of a guy that had a background in the publicity and entertainment field, so I called him. To shorten the story, we have been friends ever since with publicist Michael Laderman of 20 A-M Productions, LLC and his wife, Alyson. With his help, a new venture begins.

Today, I have a book to be published, a children's story being completed, and a stage play based on 10 years of my life called "Sheila's Waltz" that features "SIX," a medley of six of Charlie's best sax solos with Hall and Oates, and one of my songs.

As I am writing this, it is still a work in progress. But I hope I can help people to keep believing in yourself, do what you love [even if there times you want to quit] and, of course, to know we are all just passing through, hopefully to be remembered. You don't have to be famous, but a feeling of pride in what you achieve, no matter in what capacity. Meeting Charlie, having my girls, [in a few months from this writing] being grandparents for the fourth time, writing my story, having a play written about me, and creating music, I would have never thought I would get this far.

I have been so happy to fulfill one thing on my bucket list. To hear music that I wrote come to life. With help from Charlie and our good friend, Tommy Calton [an outstanding guitarist and composer], I have composed some music that I thought would be worth mentioning. A few are in the process of being recorded. You can find most of them online at CharlieDeChant.com, Charlie's official website.

My songs include "Palermo," "Don't Look Back," "Prism Sky," "Sheila's Waltz," "Tranquility," "The Outside Looking In," and "Misty Rain."

Try to relax for a moment and take in the different sounds of music from Jazz, rock, Broadway, the classics, soundtracks, etc. As long as you feel something when you hear different sounds and rhythms, you know you're connecting to people's souls. Maybe if you hear one of Charlie's CDs he recorded, you will notice a few of the songs I composed and, hopefully, enjoy my little contribution to what I love.

Life sure is full of twists and turns. But dreams sure can come true. Take care, and thank you, the reader, for reading my story.

The cast & crew of "SHEILA'S Waltz,"
L-R Charlie, me, Brianna Barrett,
Malia Henderson, Jeremy Fratti and
executive producer/writer/director
Michael Laderman.

Made in the USA
Columbia, SC
21 December 2024

50275442R00091